A GUIDE FOR NEWSPAPER STRINGERS

COMMUNICATION
TEXTBOOK SERIES
Jennings Bryant—Editor

Journalism
Maxwell McCombs—Advisor

BERNER ● Writing Literary
Features

FENSCH ● The Sports Writing
Handbook

TITCHENER ● Reviewing
the Arts

FENSCH ● Writing Solutions:
Beginnings, Middles,
and Endings

SHOEMAKER ● Communication
Campaigns about Drugs:
Government, Media,
and the Public

STEPP ● Editing for Today's
Newsroom

BOGART ● Press and Public: Who
Reads What, When, Where,
and Why in American
Newspapers, Second Edition

FENSCH ● Associated Press Coverage
of a Major Disaster: The
Crash of Delta Flight 1141

GARRISON ● Professional
Feature Writing

FENSCH ● Best Magazine
Articles: 1988

DAVIDSON ● A Guide
for Newspaper Stringers

GARRISON ● Professional
News Writing

A GUIDE FOR NEWSPAPER STRINGERS

Margaret Davidson
University of Wisconsin-Oshkosh

LEA LAWRENCE ERLBAUM ASSOCIATES, PUBLISHERS
1990   Hillsdale, New Jersey   Hove and London

Lawrence Erlbaum Associates, Inc., Publishers
365 Broadway
Hillsdale, New Jersey 07642

Library of Congress Cataloging-in-Publication Data

Davidson, Margaret F. (Margaret Ferrol), 1942–   .
   A guide for newspaper stringers / Margaret Davidson.
      p.   cm.   — (Communication textbook series)
   ISBN 0–8058–0764–0. — ISBN 0–8058–0765–9 (pbk.)
   1. Stringers (Journalists)—Handbooks, manuals, etc.   2. Reporters
and reporting—Handbooks, manuals, etc.   I. Title.   II. Series.
PN4784.S73D38   1990
070.4′3—dc20   90–2878
                                                                    CIP

Printed in the United States of America
10 9 8 7 6 5 4 3 2 1

CONTENTS

ACKNOWLEDGMENTS

As an editor directing stringers in New York state, I was struck by the tremendous desire of those correspondents to learn and grow in their job, despite the paltry pay they received for their efforts. They attended evening classes we held for them, took criticism offered in their newsletter in a professional spirit and asked me to recommend books that might help provide training.

Now as a journalism professor requested to conduct workshops for stringers, I have been amazed at the number of them willing to drive great distances to get to a workshop starting at 8 a.m. on a Saturday. And many of those people giving up their Saturdays hold down other jobs in addition to stringing.

Frequently, stringers are being called on to perform a very important professional job without any previous training or experience in the field. And they are bound and determined to learn and to do it to the best of their ability.

I would like to thank those stringers reaching out to develop their professionalism who inspired this book and who helped provide material for it. My thanks also to family and friends for valued information and support.

I would especially like to extend my appreciation to typist Judy Schultz, who miraculously translated the hieroglyphics of my final draft and with her customary professionalism accomplished the painstaking task of turning out the finished manuscript.

Grateful acknowledgment is also made to the following for the writing examples cited throughout the book:

The Associated Press
Chicago Tribune

The Denver Post
Los Angeles Times
The Miami Herald
The Milwaukee Journal
Minneapolis Star and Tribune
The New York Times
The Oshkosh Northwestern
St. Louis Post-Dispatch
USA Today
The Wall Street Journal
The Washington Post

INTRODUCTION

If a tree falls in a forest and no one hears it, is there any sound? If the mayor of Smalltown takes bribes and no reporter covers the story, is there any news?

Many Smalltown mayors can engage in questionable activity with relative immunity because no newspaper is regularly covering the area. Newsworthy events are happening daily but never become news because they are not reported. Especially in less densely populated areas of the country newspaper management may have decided it is not economical to assign reporters to cover those areas regularly.

The answer for many papers is a network of stringers who supplement the regular staff of reporters. Typically, editors make arrangements with these writers to cover a specified outlying area in the region served by their papers on a regular free-lance basis.

Those correspondents, who work from their homes covering their local areas, are the unsung heroes of the newspaper world. Often working for payment that is less than minimum wage, they report the news of their community to the world around them. Without them, those who are making significant contributions to the community may not take their rightful place in the public eye. And without them, those involved in acts detrimental to the community also are not likely to come to public attention.

Although the pay stringers typically receive is low, the job offers other significant rewards. For many it is a chance to serve their community. For others it is an opportunity to learn the journalist's trade and to get their foot in the door of a newspaper office where they might eventually be hired as a full-time reporter. Whatever their reasons for taking on the thankless task, many are turning out stories of major significance.

Take Bill White, for instance. When he was working as a stringer for the La Crosse (Wisconsin) Tribune, he provided important coverage of the Cuban immigrant situation that was among the work nominated for a Pulitzer Prize and won awards from the Inland Daily Press Association and the Milwaukee Press Club.

Fidel Castro had allowed a large number of Cubans (including, as it turned out, many dangerous misfits) to move to the United States. About 9,000 Cubans were temporarily housed at a resettlement camp set up at Fort McCoy in rural Wisconsin.

The major media rushed to the camp to cover the story. But many reporters soon returned to the cities from which they had come. Not Bill White, who lived near that remote rural area. He stayed and told the world about the stabbings and sexual assaults involving the Cubans. That stringer played an important role in uncovering the camp's problems.

Stringers' Problems

But despite their efforts, for too long stringers have been regarded as the second-class citizens of the newspaper world. They have been written off as unprofessional carriers of unimportant information about uninteresting places. Probably the Big City provincialism of metropolitan newspaper staffers is partly to blame. Too many of them think no significant news happens beyond the city limits. As a result of that shortsightedness, nuclear power plants were put up throughout the hinterlands without thorough investigation by the press. How different the coverage probably would have been had they been planned for downtown Chicago or Philadelphia or New York.

Another problem the stringer faces is the name of the position itself. It conjures up an image of a poor soul who strings along after his or her more sophisticated fellow journalists or, mayhaps, a puppet-like creature whose strings are controlled by the all-powerful editor.

Actually, the name is based on what was a common method of paying the stringer. In billing the paper, the writers cut out copies of their stories published by that paper and strung them together into one long chain. Those strings of articles were measured and the correspondents were paid for each inch of the column's length. Many stringers today are still paid based on the length of the story.

If some stringers are indeed guilty of the charge that much of what they write is unimportant, the method of pay is probably a major factor. If they are paid by the column inch it is no wonder their copy includes the latest news on Aunt

Elsie's cat, brother John's trip to Sheboygan, Mildred Hinklestein's appendectomy, the Johnson clan's family reunion and, of course, the full list of names of those who entered the pie-baking, pig-raising, and tractor-pulling contests at the farm show. Lists of names are especially lucrative. By throwing in every tidbit of gossip picked up at the supermarket, the correspondent hopes to make enough to pay for a new typewriter ribbon.

On the other hand, any story that requires time-consuming research and investigation might dwindle the stringer's pay down to pennies an hour. And if the story does not pan out, some stringers may receive no compensation at all for those many hours of work.

There is, for instance, little financial incentive for the correspondent paid by the length of the string to check out a rumor that the town's planning board members are busy buying up property that insiders say the board is about to rezone. Such a story would require the stringer to spend considerable time checking property transactions and interviewing those allegedly involved. Perhaps the rumors may turn out to be true. The story may run and the correspondent be paid—but very likely only a few dollars for many hours work. Or, after days of checking, the correspondent may find there is no substance to the rumor—no story, no pay.

When an important story is rewarded by appropriate remuneration, the quality of the stringers might well be expected to improve. Editors of many papers have come to realize this and to determine the amount of pay accordingly. Stringers are sometimes paid based on the amount of work that goes into a story. Others are now also receiving basic monthly salaries for keeping track of what is happening in their areas, even if no stories result. The practice could be expected to improve the general quality of correspondents' coverage.

Also having an effect on the quality of stringers' articles is the current job situation for journalists. The number of college graduates seeking full-time newspaper jobs far exceeds the amount of available jobs. When editors are greeted with hundreds of applications for each full-time position, they can be selective and only hire applicants with experience. As a result, even individuals with graduate degrees have taken jobs as stringers as a way of gaining newspaper experience.

Benefits of the Job

For would-be reporters, the stringer's job offers an excellent place to learn the ropes. In fact, in some ways it is a better training ground than the beginning reporter's position. The new full-time reporter is usually assigned a specialized beat. (The police beat is one of the most common assignments for rookies.) But stringers gain experience covering many areas. Police and courts, government, environment, education, business, and agriculture beats might all be among their responsibilities. The opportunity to become a competent professional skilled in covering many areas is available for the ambitious hard worker.

A stringer's job also provides writers an opportunity to show off their talents. Many stringers have been offered full-time jobs by their papers after showing what they can do. Perhaps even more frequently they have been stolen away by editors of competing papers who have seen their bylines.

Unfortunately, all too often it seems to take an outsider to appreciate their value. Editors of their own papers tend to think of stringers as nonprofessionals. It is the same problem secretaries face in trying to move up through the ranks to administrative positions. Their bosses have been geared to think of them as underlings whose values are reflected by the low rate of pay they receive, even though they might have been skillfully performing many administrative tasks. An outsider is apt to get the jobs these secretaries covet.

The stringers' problem in gaining the respect of their fellow employees at the paper and in being hired as full-time reporters is further complicated by the fact that they have so little contact with the rest of the staff. Few staffers would recognize them if they passed on the street. Generally correspondents write stories from their homes and either phone or send them in, depending on how quickly the story must appear in the paper. Rarely do they have occasion to go to the newspaper office. Their only contact with the office may be the editorial assistant to whom they dictate stories or the editor who directly supervises their work. If they are lucky, there may be an annual newspaper staff get-together to which they are invited.

This situation also makes it difficult for them to get the feedback they need on their work. Unlike their full-time counterparts, they are not likely to be greeted with the supportive "nice story" tossed out by a colleague. Nor are they around to pick up criticism about what they did wrong. Time pressures make it difficult even for the full-time reporter to get enough constructive criticism. The newspaper world is a hectic scene. As soon as one deadline is met, another one looms. There is little time to hash over past mistakes. For the stringer, who is not around the newsroom, the problem is especially serious.

This book has been prepared to help meet the stringer's need for constructive criticism. It assumes that all places are interesting and full of newsworthy activities for a professional writer with a good nose for news. The residents who live in the areas covered by stringers need to be informed about what's happening around them, and it's the stringer's responsibility to tell them—as fairly and accurately as possible.

GETTING READY TO WRITE

As a newly hired stringer, you will probably be elated about the challenge and eager to begin—but not quite sure where to start.

One of the first steps should be to make the community aware you are now the stringer for the paper. Some papers will run an article announcing new appointments and explaining how to reach you. But you should also get in touch personally with potential sources and inform them you are assuming responsibility for news coverage of the area. Your predecessor may prove helpful in suggesting useful contacts.

The former stringer may even offer to introduce those individuals to you. Let potential sources know where you can be reached. Giving out business cards with your name, phone number, address, and the name of your paper is a good way to ensure they will know how to contact you if something comes up. And it serves as a reminder to them to give you a call if something of interest happens.

Included among those to be contacted might be the fire chief, court clerk, town clerk, school board president, head of the town council, funeral directors, and the town constable. The list will, of course, vary from one area to another.

Asking these individuals for suggestions on improvement of coverage may yield good story tips. It will also show them you value their opinion, thus helping to win their confidence. Many will have an aversion to talking to representatives of the press. Perhaps they have been misquoted in the past or simply feel that what they are doing is none of the public's business. A good first impression can help you overcome some of that kind of resistance.

Keep Track of What is Happening

In addition to assisting with sources, your predecessor may have a schedule of important regular meetings and other newsworthy events happening in the area. Set up a future file to remind you of these and other important dates.

One of the easiest ways to establish such a reminder system is to take a desk calendar with a different page for each day of the year. Times of meetings, interviews, or other occurrences can be written on the calendar, and any previous stories about the topic can be attached to the page with a paper clip. Thus as you turn the page each day, you will find not only reminders of these events but also background information on them. It is important to keep an up-to-date future file. It would be difficult to explain to an irate editor why, for instance, you have missed a major confrontation between environmental groups and a paper mill at a hearing on the company's request for a permit to release polluted effluent into the river.

To make sure you are not missing out on important stories, keep abreast of news reported by others. If other papers circulate in the area, make sure you know what the competition is reporting. Ask your editor if the paper will pay for your subscriptions to the competition. Local radio and television stations should also be checked. If they beat you to a story, your editor is likely to ask why—and you better have a good answer.

National publications also provide background that is important for good local coverage. They may, for instance, report that federal legislation has been enacted calling for new kinds of subsidies to farmers. A good story might result from checking to see how farmers in your area are affected.

Helpful References

You will also need a good dictionary and a thesaurus. The experienced pro is not ashamed to be seen using these tools. The beginner especially should use them frequently. Every misspelled word causes additional work for an editor and suggests that the stringer is not careful enough. Does someone who misspells words report facts accurately, your editor might well wonder. Every mistake challenges a writer's credibility.

A thesaurus can help you find the most appropriate word. Each word has its own shade of meaning, and synonyms do not necessarily convey the same information. For instance, saying that Car A "hit" Car B suggests something different than saying Car A "collided with" Car B. The first suggests that Car A was responsible for the accident, whereas the second does not imply which, if any, is responsible. A thesaurus helps the writer find exactly the right word for the tone and meaning that needs to be conveyed.

A stylebook is another must. It sets forth rules for punctuation, usage, spelling, and other areas. Newspapers follow designated style rules to avoid inconsistencies that would make the copy appear sloppy.

In some cases, rules of grammar vary, and publications establish guidelines to determine what style will be used. For instance, some English teachers tell their students to use a comma before "and" and the last word in a series. As an example, "She bought apples, pears, and oranges." Others say leave out that last comma, thus: "She bought apples, pears and oranges." One is not necessarily more correct than another. It is a question of style. You can check your paper's stylebook and find out which form is used.

What about words that are spelled two different ways in the dictionary? Often a stylebook will cast the deciding vote.

Do you use figures or letters in reporting numbers? Which words can appropriately be abbreviated? For these and other questions you can probably find an answer by referring to your paper's stylebook.

Some papers write their own stylebooks. Many use stylebooks prepared by others. Among the most frequently consulted is *The Associated Press Stylebook and Libel Manual* (French & Goldstein, 1988). Because the wire service, which serves a large number of papers, uses that style, papers have elected to follow suit to ensure the style of their locally prepared news is the same as that which comes from AP.

It will save you wasted time and mistakes in the future if, before starting to prepare stories, you sit down and master your paper's stylebook.

Telephone directories and city directories, where they are available, are helpful in double checking names and addresses. Accuracy in reporting names is essential. Mistakes can result in some very angry and distrustful readers and possibly even a libel suit. Although complete city directories are generally too expensive to be purchased by the individual stringer, they are often available at libraries and municipal buildings as well as at newspaper offices. In addition to names, addresses, and phone numbers, they also provide information on employment of those listed.

Paperback almanacs are inexpensive and provide a wealth of background statistics. If, for instance, you are working on a story about the rash of suicides that have suddenly occurred in the town, you may want to include some national statistics on suicide. You can look up the information in the almanac.

Maps of the area are another helpful tool. You may find them available at local municipal buildings or real estate offices at little or no cost. Regional planning offices are also good sources for maps, including a number of specialized types. Maps are frequently needed for checking on locations of stories. Sometimes you may want to determine the site of a story in relation to a familiar landmark. Describing the location in these terms will help the reader understand where it is.

Typing Format

The most important tool of the trade is, of course, the typewriter or perhaps the computer. All copy submitted in written form to the newspaper should be typed. Newspaper staff members are too busy to waste time deciphering a stringer's handwritten scribblings.

Although each newspaper has its own guidelines, many ask reporters to start the first page of copy about one third of the way down the paper. Space is left at the top of the page for instructions on headlines, on what page the copy is to be used or other information the editor needs to provide on handling of the story. Subsequent pages of the copy start about 1 inch from the top of the page.

Leave about a 1-inch margin at the bottom of the page. If the story continues on the next page, write "-more-" centered under the last line to alert the editor and typesetter to look for the rest of the article. Use "-30-" centered under the last line to indicate the end of the story. Unless the editor gives other instructions, leave about 1 inch each for the left and the right margins. Size of these margins tends to vary with the size of the letters produced by the typewriter. Many editors find that their job of laying out pages is facilitated if their reporters set their margins so that 1 inch of typewritten copy equals 1 inch of type in a newspaper column. They may instruct you what margin to set on your typewriter to make this possible.

Use a new sheet of paper for each separate story. Every article should have a "slug" to identify it. A slug is a label used on each page of the story. For instance, a story about the derailment of a train that resulted in the death of 15 people might be slugged "Train." It is placed at the top left of the page. Under it goes the reporter's last name. Many papers also require the date. Thus at the top left of a page of copy you might have the following:

Train

Smith

10–22–90

If the story is more than one page long, indicate the page order of succeeding pages by following the slug with the word "add" and the number of the page added. For instance, the second page of the train derailment story would be labeled "Train—add 1." The third page would be "Train—add 2" and so on. This style varies somewhat from one newspaper to another.

Always double space typewritten copy. When you are making revisions, you will find you need that extra line for additions and corrections. Editors, too, need to have room to make changes.

Editing Symbols

Journalists have a shorthand method of indicating changes to the copy. Among the most frequently used are the symbols illustrated here:

The accident occured at the ist corner of Fifth and Ohio Streets. police said the driver of the truck been has charged with drunken driving.

He is John Smith, twenty, of 15 Pa Avenue. He also faces 2 other charges related to the incident, police said. stated

He is scheduled to appear in court on July 7.

Here's what they mean:

The—indent

acci**d**ent—change a letter

occur**c**ed—add a letter (a word can also be added this way)

ist—delete

Sixth
Fifth—change the word

;—delete letter or punctuation mark to which the tail-like symbol is attached

Streets—change to lower case the capital letter with the line through it

police—capitalize the letter under which the three lines have been drawn

driver—transpose the letters indicated

been has—transpose the words indicated

twenty—use Arabic numbers instead of the word to express the number

Pa—substitute the full form for the abbreviation

Avenue—abbreviate the word indicated by the circle

2—write out in word form

other charges—add a space

incident—close up space

police—add a comma

stated
said—ignore correction

said—add a period

other charges related to the incident, police said.

He is—no new paragraph

The revised copy, after the changes indicated are made, would read as follows:

> The accident occurred at the corner of Sixth and Ohio streets. Police said the driver of the truck has been charged with drunken driving.
>
> He is John Smith, 20, of 15 Pennsylvania Ave. He also faces two other charges related to the incident, police said. He is scheduled to appear in court on July 7.

Handling Expenses

Many papers will provide the stringer with "copy paper," which is a low-grade, relatively inexpensive paper used in printing newspapers. Some will also supply stamped envelopes for sending in copy. Others will ask stringers to use their own envelopes and stamps and keep track of their mailing costs. Telephone and travel expenses may also be reimbursed.

When in doubt about what is expected, don't hesitate to ask your supervising editor.

KEEPING AN EYE OUT
FOR NEWS

A good writer is a good observer—of people, surroundings, ideas and trends, and the general flotsam and jetsam of the world around.

Some people seem to go through life with blinders on. They are so wrapped up in their own comings and goings they are unaware of the ebb and flow around them. But others observe the world in sharp detail with the vision to see everything in perspective, appreciating its true value.

I have become especially conscious of the difference in outlook between various individuals in the years I have been teaching college journalism. For some of the students in the reporting classes, the world seems to be a colorful and fascinating place with an endless supply of worthwhile news stories. But for many others it appears to be a very sterile, boring existence where little that is exciting ever happens. Constantly they need help in coming up with ideas for stories.

To a large extent, the quality of a writer's work is dependent on his or her perception of the world. Some of the best journalists look out into that world with the eyes of a child—ever questioning, ever wondering at its mysteries.

Have you noticed a difference in coverage when a new reporter takes over a beat of your local newspaper? The former reporter may have been a very skillful journalist, but it is extremely hard to preserve that freshness of vision when you have been covering the same area for years. Although new reporters approach the task with the disadvantage of lacking the experience and knowledge of the area enjoyed by their predecessors, they come with the advantage of more easily being able to see the subject area through eyes similar to their readers'.

Nor does it matter much what the subject of coverage is. The religion beat can produce as many significant stories as the government beat in the hands of the right reporter.

Finding News on a Beat

Take the way Dennis McCann approached his new task of covering the agriculture beat for *The Milwaukee Journal,* for instance. On a large portion of the days of the week you could find McCann stories either on the front page or the main local page of the *Journal.* Let's look at how he handled his beat during one 2-month period.

One of his tricks is that he knows how to get the most out of the apparently routine story that has to be covered even if it is not likely to be high in news value.

For the agriculture reporter on *The Milwaukee Journal* one such mandatory story is the state fair. If you have spent much time at fairs, you know that although they may be high drama for those who have entered their rabbits and pies and flower arrangements, they do not exactly have the excitement of a Watergate when it comes to news value.

But McCann's keen eye came to his rescue. He noticed the tears of sadness of the little 9-year-old as the prize-winning steer he had lovingly nurtured with his 15-year-old brother was sold for the high bid of $13,750. And his touching feature effectively told the bittersweet tale of the victory.

Another McCann fair story reported on the first Wisconsin–Illinois Battle of the States whose skirmishes included an udder contest, cow-chip throw, and liar's competition. (First-ever stories are often a good bet.)

And he remembers his audience and their needs. Farming is big business in Wisconsin, the dairy state. Not only are the many readers involved in farming interested in the business of agriculture but also citizens throughout the state who appreciate its role as one of Wisconsin's major industries. If farmers are in a financial squeeze, their plight is likely to be shared by the farm-equipment dealers who sell them their tractors, the bankers who loan them their money, and the state taxpayers who depend on their contributions to the state coffers.

And so McCann wrote a story on Friends of the Family Farm, a group that strives to help small- and medium-sized farms. And he did another feature on the farm cooperatives' need to restrict credit.

He also covered meetings where important news on the business of farming might develop. Coverage of the state Assembly Subcommittee on Rural Economic Development yielded a significant story on the perceived need to change federal tax laws to remove from agricultural classification those individuals who are more interested in lowering their tax liabilities than raising crops. "Cold, hard doctors' cash" has driven up land values and farm costs, one participant charged.

A hearing conducted by the state Department of Agriculture, Trade and Consumer Protection turned up another important issue. Farmers and soil conservationists called for changes to help prevent soil erosion that has been plaguing the state. Voluntary programs have failed, they charged, and called for economic incentives to help farmers install soil-saving measures.

Another meeting, the joint convention of the Midwest and Wisconsin Dairy Products associations, turned up some ideas for Wisconsin dairy farmers that might be borrowed from an expert from another state. An official of the California Milk Advisory Board told participants they must develop new milks for new times if they are to compete successfully in the high-stakes market.

He described a proposal Californians were working on to produce various kinds of milk. Super milk would be super-enriched and aimed at active, sports-minded young people. Slim milk—low in fat but not in protein—would be used to try to appeal to the active but weight-conscious adults. And for older adults, a milk low in fat and cholesterol but still containing plenty of vitamins.

This kind of suggestion for handling of a reader's problems is an important addition to a newspaper page. Critics of the media rightfully charge that we are too likely to stress problems without helping to come up with information on possible solutions to those problems. Taking a look at how a problem is being dealt with elsewhere makes a valuable contribution to readers concerned about the issue.

McCann also recognizes the value of surveys done by others. Often someone with expertise in the area has put a lot of work into finding out about issues of newsworthy interest that a typical rushed reporter would not have the time to explore. Make use of the legwork of those experts.

One such survey McCann reported on was prepared by the state's Department of Agriculture, Trade and Consumer Protection. It came up with some startling findings about the business of farming. According to the survey results, more than one third of Wisconsin farmers indicated they expected to be out of the business within 5 years of the time the survey was conducted if the economic conditions did not improve.

And *The Milwaukee Journal* farm reporter had a sharp eye peeled for the unusual and just plain interesting. Thus was hatched the story on the strange fowl produced by crossing a chicken with a pheasant. In the *Journal* article McCann describes how the piece on "Why did a chicken cross a pheasant?" happened to be written. The original call was made to Ed Tafelski Jr., who had been featured on the front page of the *Mellen Weekly Record*. The farmer was pictured standing above a tranquilized black bear that had attacked him while he was feeding his pigs. The reporter wanted to interview him about the attack.

But the misdirected phone call instead turned up his uncle, Ted Tafelski, who identified himself as "the one that's got the crossed chickens and pheasants."

What do you do as a journalist if you find yourself in this kind of situation? The answer is a true test of how good a reporter you really are.

Some writers are so rigid and inflexible that in their dogged determination to finish up their envisioned story, they fail to see leads for other articles or new paths for their original story developing along the way.

And some are afraid to deviate and pursue the unusual. No matter that you may not have read anywhere else about such a strange crossbreeding. And no matter that there is a distinct possibility Uncle Ted might just be a kook. Check it out and see where the story leads you. Nothing ventured, nothing gained. For McCann, it led to a front-page story.

His vision is 20–20. McCann, now a *Journal* columnist, could see the small, often unnoticed details, like the tears of the fair champion's keeper. But at the same time he was well aware of the big picture of his beat that stretched beyond the lush pastures of Wisconsin to, for instance, the lawmakers in Washington who would be deciding on taxes that affect the local farmers and the California dairymen who would be competing with them.

He took a beat that many reporters would avoid like the plague because they fear their articles will end up at the back of the paper buried next to the obituaries. But in his competent hands the area he was covering often instead ended up on the front page.

Nor did he have to be amid the glow of the big-city lights to come up with good stories. Many of his datelines were from places like Mellen, population 1,046—the small towns and villages that dot a large portion of the Wisconsin road map.

Big Stories From Small Towns

Important news is everywhere. The daily happenings of a small town are a microcosm of what is going on throughout the country. Issues attracting national attention are affecting the daily lives in Smalltown, U.S.A.

Take these examples, for instance: A string of neighbors are distressed to find their wells have been contaminated with gasoline, perhaps from a leaking underground tank at a long-ago abandoned gas station, as experts throughout the land warn that our groundwater supply is in jeopardy. A planned downtown convention-center project, which the city fathers had hoped would save their withering downtown, is threatened with financial disaster as congressmen mull over possible legislative changes providing for tax incentives that would help such projects get off the ground. The concern over the congressional action is shared by municipal officials in every state.

We too often forget the value of covering carefully the grass-roots effect of state and federal legislation. Newspapers place some of their highest paid, most experienced reporters on the task of covering state and federal governments. An assignment to the state capital or Washington is a coveted challenge, and well it should be. But often it is up to the stringers to keep an eye out for the local ramifications of that much-discussed legislation that is too often forgotten about once it leaves the desk of the governor or president.

Does the new state groundwater legislation really contribute to a solution of the problem by helping to identify the source of the pollution and preventing further contamination? What effect are the tax credits to encourage revitalizing old buildings having on commercial and residential areas throughout the nation?

But be forewarned. Sometimes it takes more guts to cover smaller areas than it does the national scene. I cannot remember ever having anyone call up to react to a story I did the whole summer I worked for national columnist Jack Anderson. And those stories were heard or read by hundreds of thousands who watched Anderson's reports on ABC's "Good Morning America" or read his newspaper columns.

But write something for a little weekly newspaper and watch out. Be prepared to defend what you said at the local supermarket or baseball game. Those are your neighbors you are writing about, and they will let you know if they like the story—or don't. My experience has been, the larger the news organization for which you write, the less feedback from readers, and that may be part of the reason why many experienced writers prefer to cover the smaller areas.

No matter what size area you are assigned to cover, if you have a sharp eye for news, there will be more good story possibilities out there than you can begin to handle.

Let's assemble a checklist that will help you in coming up with worthwhile news stories.

News Checklist

Look for the significant

A story that has a considerable effect on a substantial number of people is apt to have major significance. For instance, information that toxic substances dumped into the river by local industries are poisoning fish to the extent that the state is suggesting fish-eaters limit their consumption is significant. Many are affected, and the effect, sadly, may turn out to be substantial.

The new municipal budget and the resulting tax rate are likely to be very significant stories for local papers. Everyone—homeowners and tenants, school teachers and their pupils, street repairers and commuters—are affected by the taxes of a community.

And be careful to explain the significance of a story to your readers. What health hazards can result from eating contaminated fish? How much in additional taxes will the new tax rate mean for the owner of a $75,000 home?

Report on the unusual

If a chicken mates with another chicken, the event just has the makings of another barnyard romance. But if a chicken mates with a pheasant—that is news.

As an editor of a paper in Western New York, I once had a grandmotherly looking stringer who had a fascinating eye for news. Ruth Fees had just started on her journalistic journey at her more advanced age, but she seemed to view the world with a childlike wonder.

From her typewriter came the story of a man who annually floated down the river on his back, pulling his boat behind him. Her story on whether cows produced more milk if they listened to classical or rock music never quite materialized, but the research she did on panhandling did pan out. Her request for dimes would have yielded her quite a take (had she not returned the loot from kindly contributors). On the other hand, when she tried to give money away, she had no takers. For her, there were plenty of unusual happenings in the sparsely populated area she covered.

Remember your audience, find the local angle

If you are writing for a New Jersey newspaper, your readers will not share a Wisconsin reader's interest in udders and cow chips.

To understand the needs of your community, become a vital part of it. Many professional journalists are criticized because they spend so much time with each other, they are unaware of the reading needs of the general community. They too often write to please their fellow journalists and not the reading public. That kind of attitude can contribute to the arrogance with which we in the media have been charged.

Always look for a local angle for a story. For instance, localize a story on the proposed revisions in federal income taxes by getting your local congressman to comment on the plan.

Remember your paper's total circulation base. If you are stringing for a newspaper with a countywide audience, be especially on the lookout for stories involving county facilities in the area for which you are responsible. County parks, hospitals and airports, for instance, often are fodder for good news stories.

And if you are stringing for a statewide paper, watch out for the state prisons, parks, mental-health institutions, and other state property.

Read widely and become aware of what is going on in the world

A good journalist needs a broad knowledge of what is happening to be able to recognize when something is news. Is it a unique occurrence? Is it, perhaps, the beginning of a trend?

And many times you need background information to be able to understand what is being said or is happening. If you have not kept well-enough informed, you can be in big trouble. The governor may speak in your area or a state legislative hearing is held there, for instance, and you as the local stringer have to cover those events. If you are uninformed about state issues, you are likely to have trouble providing clear and thorough coverage.

And the same thing is true of national background. Try to read at least one newsmagazine a week and a national paper like *The New York Times* each day.

My favorite source of background information is *The Wall Street Journal*. The *Journal* is well ahead of many of the media in spotting trends—and it does a fine job of documenting them, explaining them, and suggesting their possible ramifications. A large portion of news media are pack journalists, jumping on stories others have already reported about. The *Journal* is frequently leading the pack.

Borrow ideas from what is being reported on nationally. If the administration is being accused of cutting back on food services to the poor, report on the business being done by your local soup kitchen. Check to see if any of the churches are responding in an unusual way in trying to meet the needs of the poor.

But be aware that your editor may want you to cover a response such as this only if it is unique to the geographic area you are assigned to cover. Otherwise a full-time reporter is likely to be assigned to do such a story, either concentrating on the municipality where the paper enjoys its largest circulation or combining information from areas throughout the regions where the paper circulates.

Watch what your competitors in the local media are doing. Keep track of what all the other newspapers and radio and television stations are reporting on. If they have an important news story that you have missed, you had better round up information on it as quickly as possible.

Come up with ways to update a story that your competitors have already had or approach it from a different angle. Think creatively. What source might you talk to in addition to their sources? What are the ramifications of a story? What interesting human angle might be reported on?

Generate effective sources

The county clerk, district attorney, police chief, school principal, city manager, local developer, head of the county medical association, hospital administrator . . . and the list goes on and on . . . all are important sources of ideas for stories.

Check with key sources on a regular basis to see if anything of newsworthy interest is happening. And when you are interviewing a source for information on a particular story, ask if anything else of interest is going on. In some cases request that they give you a call if something develops. Many, like a district attorney running for re-election, will be very happy to alert you to such news.

Keep your eyes open

A billboard suddenly goes up asking citizens not to patronize certain listed businesses because they hire non-union labor. That is a story.

A for sale sign goes up on property that had been sold for a major new development. Look into it.

Dozens of dead fish wash up on the river's banks. Time to get to work.

As you become an expert on your area after writing many stories about it, you will find an increasing number of sights will send you back to the typewriter. Look carefully and think about the ramifications of what you are seeing.

Get yourself put on mailing lists to receive press releases and notifications of meetings in your area

Among those you might want to ask to send you such information are:

- Your local state and congressional representatives,
- County and municipal governmental bodies,
- The local chamber of commerce,
- The school board,
- Colleges and technical schools, and
- Regional planning bodies.

Some of these, such as the legislators and the universities, may have staff people whose full-time job is providing information for the media.

Many states have open-meeting laws that require government bodies to notify media representatives who have requested such information about their upcoming meetings. In some cases you may have to submit a written request for that notification.

Often the notices will include an agenda so you can get an idea whether the meeting is something you should cover. Sometimes those notices may give you ideas for feature stories buried amid the routine listings.

Take this list of items on the agenda of a meeting scheduled by a county Agriculture and Extension Education Committee, for instance: ball diamonds at the fairgrounds; County Fair report; Fair Association operational budget; community garden budget; natural beautification budget; Farm Progress Days budget. What feature possibilities does it offer?

Perhaps several possibilities may have come to mind. But one that looks like an especially good bet is a story on the community garden. Without having read the agenda notice, you might never even have known that such a garden exists.

The subject has news value.

For most areas, such a garden is unusual in these times. And the idea of people working together at their gardening hobby has special human appeal. Furthermore, you may find the story has further significance, once you start looking into it. Was the garden perhaps started during the recessionary times when many people strapped for money were finding it hard to buy all the food their families needed? Can fewer people in the community afford single-family housing and the plots of land that go with them resulting in more of an interest in community gardening? Are there more single individuals in the community who are looking for a wholesome interest to share with others?

Checking into this garden would have revealed that a considerable portion of the sites were being nurtured by Southeast Asian refugees, many of whom had been farmers in their native Laos before being driven out by the Communists in retaliation for their aid to the United States.

Press releases may yield similar kinds of feature possibilities. Something only barely mentioned in the release may turn out to be a focus for a story.

Remember that journalists have a responsibility not just to handle well the stories they write but also to make sure they cover news that needs to be reported upon within the areas of their responsibility

Stringing arrangements will differ from one paper to another. Perhaps you are fortunate enough to be working for a paper which clearly delineates the responsibilities of each stringer. If so, you have probably been assigned a specific geographic area that you and you alone are responsible for covering.

On the other hand, perhaps you are working for a paper with overlapping stringers and no one is sure who is responsible for doing what. If so, you might want to try to work out an arrangement with the supervising editor or with the other stringers in your area to set guidelines of responsibilities. This will prevent writers from wasting their time on overlapping coverage. Perhaps each might like to handle certain sections of the area or you might want to divide up the beats by subject with one person, for instance, covering government and police news and another covering education and the environment.

Once you know your area of responsibility, try to make sure you are covering the important news within it. Failure to do so can cause serious problems for the readers depending upon your paper. If, for instance, there is a prison within your area from which a number of inmates have escaped, a story will need to be done on how the escapes occurred and what is being done to prevent future problems.

If a certain railroad crossing has been the scene of all too many fatal accidents, dig into it. Yes, it will take longer than a quick feature on a local dollmaker, but remember such time-consuming stories are an important part of your responsibility.

Work Efficiently

And so there are a seemingly unlimited number of ideas for stories. It is a good approach to have several ideas to work on at one time to avoid wasting time. Often there will be a delay in getting one of the stories together. Perhaps a main source is at a meeting or for some other reason is unavailable at the moment. Or maybe it will take some time for your sources to round up the information you need. In the meantime, start working on one of your other story ideas.

Also to avoid wasting time, check out your ideas for stories with your editor before beginning to work on the articles. Usually a news staffer called a state, area, or regional editor is in charge of stringers and other journalists covering the outlying area beyond the home base of the paper.

Especially until you get more familiar with that editor and learn what he or she wants, you may find yourself writing a story that individual views as having no news value if you do not get a go-ahead before proceeding. The story is not run and you have wasted your time. Or perhaps the paper has already done a story on that subject. Again your article goes in the circular file.

Once you have approval for the story but it just does not pan out, many editors will pay you for the time you invested in the research.

You might want to come up with a list of a dozen or so ideas to run by your editor, especially when you first assume your new stringing job. Your editor's comments on which are good possibilities will help you to understand the paper's needs. Carefully studying the other articles in the paper and how they are placed will also assist you in understanding the value that is placed on various kinds of news at that particular publication.

The generation of ideas is a sort of creative brainstorming. You are likely to find that the more you write about things in your community, the more there seems to be to write about. In fact, it is not the lack of story ideas but the lack of time to get around to all of them that may well turn out to be your biggest problem.

JOURNALISTIC STYLE

Before trying to master any skill, it is a good idea to step back and try to figure out what you need to accomplish. What is the goal, the mission?

Until you determine that, you can waste a lot of time spinning your wheels. And despite the additional time you expend, your product may be less than perfect.

For a carpenter, an important goal is that the end result be strong and lasting. And it must be aesthetically pleasing. Good proportions and well-crafted finish are important.

The writer, too, is a craftsman. He or she is building ideas and images and blocks of information by hammering together words and phrases. The goal is communication with strong substance and aesthetically pleasing style.

But the style of communication varies depending on exactly what the word-smith is trying to accomplish. The mission of a preacher attempting to inspire his flock, for instance, is very different from a novelist spinning a good yarn. The political speechwriter, the essayist, the poet—all are communicating with words, but their objectives are different and thus, so too, are their styles.

What, then, is the object of the journalist? When you as a stringer are constructing with words, what are you trying to accomplish? What special factors must you take into consideration when writing for a newspaper? Here are some suggestions.

Style Hints

Write tightly and directly

Limited space is a major consideration. A lot of information must be crammed into the newspaper, and to help your editors work in that news, write tightly. Each day, the newspaper staff has determined its news hole—that is, the amount of space available for news content. Usually the calculation is made by first computing the extent of advertising to be run because ads pay for a large portion of the newspaper's bills. Once the ad tally is known, a determination can be made as to how much news space will be available. A typical ratio used as a guideline by papers is 60-40, with advertising accounting for 60% of the space and the rest devoted to the news hole.

Some days of the week are generally bigger advertising days than others. Wednesday and Sunday papers tend to have the most ads in many towns.

As a result, some days your editor will have more room for your stories than others. Watch the size of a typical paper each day of the week to get an idea of when space is most plentiful.

The amount of news competing with your story will also have a great effect on how much space is available for your articles. In many areas that news stream can be counted on to ebb and flow with the days of the week. Often Monday and Saturday papers tend to have relatively less news competing for space because things have wound down in the workaday world on the preceding Fridays and Sundays.

As a result, you are likely to find that a story with average news value may receive a lot bigger play on a Monday, for instance, than on other days of the week. And your editor may be more likely to use a longer feature on that day.

You might want to check with your editor to see how tight space is before cranking out a long news story. But in journalistic writing, more is not necessarily better. Direct, tight writing is the mark of a good journalist.

That is not to say that you should skimp on including sufficient facts. Quite the contrary. One of the major advantages newspapers have over the popular electronic media is their ability to explore news in greater depth.

But communicate those facts efficiently. Not only is space limited, but a typical newspaper reader only has limited time during the day to devote to a daily newspaper. Readers need to find out what is happening in their local community as well as throughout the world. They need a lot of information quickly, and they are turning to the newspaper to serve it up for them.

Their expectations are very different than if they were to sit down to read a book or a magazine. They are likely to be approaching such reading in a more leisurely manner. The author's style should be adjusted accordingly. Flourishes, lengthy descriptions, and a more personal style, for instance, are more likely to find a place in a book or a magazine. And if that is the kind of writing you prefer, perhaps you should reconsider your job as a stringer. As a newspaper correspondent, you are not often permitted the luxury of such techniques.

Be as objective as possible

Unlike an essayist, as a newspaper article writer you are not at liberty to espouse a cause. That is not to say that as a journalist you cannot perform an important social function and help reshape your corner of the world. Indeed, just by selecting a story to write about, you are able to make a difference.

Perhaps you are concerned about the quality of the local schools. OK, do a story on the situation. Compile information on standardized tests scores, opinions of students, teachers, administrators, parents, and alumni. But do not include your own opinion. A statement like "Hometown schools are in big trouble" does not belong in a news story, unless, of course, it is attributed to a source who has made the charge. We must bend over backward to be as objective as possible.

Nonetheless, there is perhaps no way we can defend ourselves against our critics who charge that newspapers lack objectivity. Just by selecting news, organizing a story with the main emphasis first, and deciding how the story should be played in the paper, we are making a value judgment. And to that extent a newspaper is a subjective creation. It is a product of the backgrounds of the journalists who create it and make the judgments.

But in the manner in which we gather the information for news articles and write it up, we need to strive to be as objective as possible. We must be well enough informed that we know when there is not just another side which we should present on an issue but, as is often the case, several other sides.

And we must take a neutral stance in our writing style. That means that almost never should you be writing stories in the first person. Instead, place the spotlight on others.

Indeed, there are those rare occasions when it is appropriate to use the first person. If you yourself have become part of the unfolding news story, your editor will usually agree to a first-person approach. For instance, when Bernice Huxtable, then a stringer for the *Niagara Gazette,* got a job as an extra in a movie being made at Niagara Falls, first-person was an appropriate device. Because she was herself a part of the movie, her personal experiences, told in her wonderfully colorful personal style, worked well in describing the movie's production to readers. But if she had just been on the set as an observer reporting on what others were doing, first-person would not have been appropriate.

It is a good idea to check with your editor for permission before writing anything in first person. Editors are constantly on guard against showboating writers trying to interject their own personalities in inappropriate ways. They will be able to help you decide if you have indeed come across the rare instance when you can use the usually forbidden "I" and "we."

Usually editors go out of their way to remove such first-person pronouns from news copy. A good copy editor will not even let words like "our country" or "our economy" get into print unless they are part of a direct quote. Nor is any reference to the reporter writing the story likely to stay. Similarly, generally avoid subjective adjectives like "interesting," "tragic," or "phenomenal." Give your readers the facts and let them decide themselves which subjective descriptions are appropriate. However, be aware that the latitude allowed by editors regarding such style restrictions will vary between papers and even between various sections of the same paper. And, of course, editorial and column writers are not bound by the same rules of objectivity. Read carefully and analytically the style of the section for which you are writing to determine what is considered appropriate.

Simplify, simplify

Remember the wide range of readers who will be reading your articles. Make them understandable even for those with only an eighth-grade education. You are not writing a treatise for the erudite. You are relaying information for the general citizens who value the paper's role in helping them to be well-informed.

So use as simple words as possible. Perhaps you too passed through the stage I went through when as a ninth grader I first started writing compositions. A real budding intellectual—remember those days? To try to make my silly little essays sound really learned, I took the simple words and substituted the most highfaluting verbiage I could find.

I was playing the game backward. As a communicator, the simplest words work the best. And so do simple sentences and paragraphs.

In many instances you may find yourself in the role of a translator—taking the convoluted expressions of the lawyer, the academician, the bureaucrat, perhaps, and transforming them into words that the average reader can understand. Get rid of the jargon, the pretentious phrases.

Sometimes it can be a struggle, almost like translating a foreign language. Here, for instance, are the guidelines of an academician written in academese. I think his goal, ironically, was to seek to improve communication at the university, but it is hard to know for sure. "The Academic Systems and University Information Programs and Services divisions will seek to improve articulation between their materials production services (photo-graphics, radio and television) leading toward improved functioning and productivity through a single project management structure." Huh?

Somehow various institutions and disciplines seem to generate their own language that isolates outsiders. Critics raise interesting questions about the motivation for doing so. If the legalese of contracts and other documents were more easily understood by the laymen, would the lawyers' services be needed as often? Are academicians perhaps making their area of specialty seem more complicated and impressive by their erudite-sounding verbiage?

Whatever their motivation, we as journalists must cut through the claptrap. One of our major functions is to serve as a bridge between the specialists and the rest of society so that we can all share equally in their advances. That can be much more difficult than it sounds. First-rate journalists make it look so easy. Their writing seems so simple and easy to understand that the general public often does not appreciate the tremendous amount of work that went into digesting a complicated subject so thoroughly that the article about it can be understood by any reader.

Take the way Marilyn Chase of *The Wall Street Journal* led us slowly and patiently to an understanding of AIDS (acquired immune deficiency syndrome) virus. She wrote:

> Invisible to ordinary microscopes, the supposed AIDS virus is only 1/80 the size of a single red blood cell. It does not eat or breathe and—consisting simply of genes inside a protein "coat"—lives only to spawn copies of itself. For this, it invades the cells of its victim and multiplies. . . .
>
> Under an electron microscope, AIDS virus looks like a sphere wrapped in protein, much as a candy apple is coated with caramel and nuts. On the outside are nuggets of a substance called glycoprotein, clinging to a caramel-like layer called transmembrane protein. . . .

Sometimes, as in the paragraph just cited, complicated concepts can best be explained by comparing them to something in our everyday experience. This device can be especially effective in suggesting the significance or magnitude of something. For instance, a reader could be helped to appreciate the size of an aircraft carrier by comparing it to the length of a certain number of football fields.

Strive for crispness and clarity. If your words seem to be tripping over themselves and your sentences awkward, you have problems. Do not try to convey too many diverse ideas in a single sentence. The solution may be breaking one long sentence down into two shorter ones.

If you are accustomed to other styles of writing, newspaper style may at first seem very choppy indeed. Especially the length of paragraphs may be disconcerting because rarely does a newspaper paragraph contain more than three or four sentences. And many are made up only of one lone sentence.

By limiting the amount of information in a paragraph to closely related subject matter, the journalist increases the clarity of the writing. Shorter paragraphs also have a positive effect on the appearance of the newspaper page. Because columns of newspaper type are relatively narrow, paragraphs extend down the page farther and can appear longer than when spread across a wider width, as in a book. As a result, a column with few paragraphs is likely to look gray and forbidding and hard to read. The white space produced when new paragraphs are indented helps to break up those long columns of type.

Be precise

Every word must convey precisely the exact meaning needed in the situation. We are working with an exceptionally versatile language. English abounds with words that have similar meanings. Yet in most cases the meanings are not exactly the same. We must select the one that works just right.

Take this example. Which verb would you select to best get the point across in the following sentence?

> A survey (discloses, implies, reveals, shows, suggests, indicates) that 58% of Smalltown residents attend church regularly.

Watch out for "discloses" and "reveals." They suggest that someone had clandestinely swept something under the rug and the information is now at last out in the open. The reporter on an ego trip is tempted to use such words to enhance his or her own self-importance. Indeed, such words are appropriate if hidden information is being revealed, but otherwise try for a more appropriate verb.

What about "suggests"? No, not definite enough. And "implies" suffers from a similar problem.

That leaves us with a choice of "shows" or "indicates." A major difference between the two is that "shows" seems more definite than "indicates." How definite should the tone be in this case? Because in most surveys, only a portion of the population is questioned, the percentage figure may be off a bit. Therefore, "indicates" would be a better choice here.

Be aware, for instance, that there is a difference between a robbery and a burglary, a lawyer and an attorney, a boycott and an embargo. When in doubt about the exact meaning of words, look them up. *The Associated Press Stylebook and Libel Manual* is especially helpful in explaining such distinctions.

Be equally precise in the information you provide. Collect the specifics. Do not refer to a middle-aged woman, for instance, but rather to a 38-year-old woman. Do not refer to Jane Dornan of the Department of Health but rather to Jane Dornan, assistant secretary of the Department of Health. Admittedly it takes a lot more time to collect such specifics, but that is part of your job. Anything less is sloppy, imprecise reporting.

Try to hold the reader's attention

We are faced with an information explosion. Your story is competing with many other bits of information for the reader's attention. If it is to serve its intended function of communicating, it must be read.

You may enjoy writing just for the sake of writing. Indeed, you may even find it therapeutic. But good journalistic writing is intended to go beyond that personal satisfaction. When you write for a newspaper, write to be read.

To do so, remember your reader. How would you tell a friend about information you are writing up for the paper? Often that method of relating the facts may work well in writing the article.

Be a collector of attention grabbers. Look for the colorful tidbit, the revealing anecdote, the exciting quote. Work them effectively into the story.

And think carefully about how much information should be included. Some good writers say they may include only half of the material they have collected for their article. They discard the rest because it only bogs down the story.

No matter how good a writer you are, your story can only be as good as the information you have collected. You need that material as building blocks. If you have been lazy in gathering the information, your story will crumble and fall apart.

Good journalistic writing, like many skills, is an effective combination of style and substance. Unless you use an effective style, the reader is likely to misunderstand the facts or fail to appreciate their significance. And the story may not be read at all.

But strong substance is also crucial. Even with words that sing and phrases that seem to flow effortlessly from the typewriter, without the substance, the piece conveys little of value to the reader.

THE LEAD IS HALF
THE BATTLE

How to start? That blank piece of paper looks so very blank when you sit down to type up the bits and pieces of information you have painstakingly compiled. And the more there is of that information, the harder it seems to get rolling.

But once you find the right lead, the rest of the story often unfolds as if it had a life of its own.

However, coming up with that lead can be a difficult challenge. Even the most experienced pros can start to fill up a wastebasket with their rejected attempts. And in fact, often the more experienced the writer, the fuller the wastebasket. A skillful writer is painfully aware of the vital importance of a good lead.

When I have been asked to review stringers' copy in preparation for workshops I have conducted for them, unsuccessful leads have been the single biggest problem I have encountered.

Let's forget about the old advice to try to work in the who, what, when, where, how, and why into every lead. Following that suggestion may make the lead too long and unwieldy. And rigidly adhering to that guideline can distract you from keeping in mind more important goals.

Those goals will vary with the nature of the story. Often you will be trying to find a lead that will work with a straightforward hard news story about specific events or occurrences, such as an account of a town meeting or a fire. That sort of article needs a lead that will get at the most significant news as smoothly and efficiently as possible.

Lead Suggestions

Here are some suggestions to keep in mind.

Look for the newsworthy

The trick is figuring out what is the most newsworthy, the most interesting part of the information you have collected. And doing so gets back to the same concerns discussed in the chapter on how to spot news. Look for information that is significant because of its wide-ranging effect, the unusual, the colorful, the indicator of a trend.

Don't back into it

Once you have decided on the information that belongs in the lead, organize it in a way that gets directly at the main focus. Don't back into it. Problems with backing into the information may arise, for instance, if a writer begins the lead with when the happening occurred or starts off with a prepositional phrase. Here is an example of a focus problem caused by reporting the time first: "Last night the City Council voted to shut down the massage parlors."

Avoid topic leads

Check to make sure you have not used a label or topic lead that is too general because it merely refers to the overall subject. Look at the difference between a lead with true news value and a topic lead that does not really tell the reader anything new. For example, "Assemblyman Percy Thompson spoke on the topic of state taxes Monday night."

Revised, the lead reads, "Assemblyman Percy Thompson charged Monday night that the state's tax structure penalizes middle-income taxpayers."

Imagine the job faced by the editor trying to write a headline based on your lead. If it contains nothing newsworthy that might make an interesting headline, the shortcoming of the first example, you no doubt have problems.

Emphasize the latest developments

Whenever appropriate, work in a time element that shows the reader the story is timely. One of the main goals in the media game is to present current, timely stories and to beat the competition to those stories. As a result, editors strive to make their stories appear as up to date as possible. To help stress that timeliness, your lead will usually mention when the news took place.

For instance:

Hurricane Carol blasted into the Florida coast today with 100 mph winds, collapsing seaside cottages and flooding streets.

About 100 more local families are on general relief this year than last year, according to a report released today by the Department of Social Services.

Including the day when the report is released makes it appear current. Generally, papers concentrate largely on events that took place since the previous paper came out. As a result, a weekly newspaper focuses heavily on the events of the week prior to publication and a daily on the happenings within the last day.

But sometimes reporters may not learn of the happening in time for the current issue or are unable to get the information written up by that time for other reasons. Yet it is still of real news value and they want to inform their readers about the story.

Frequently their solution is to attempt to update the story and make it as current as possible. For instance, say a local resident was killed in a plane crash in a different part of the country, but the paper in his hometown only heard about the accident 3 days after the happening. The story about the crash might begin with a lead like this, which focuses attention on what is happening today.

Federal authorities are continuing today to investigate the cause of the plane crash in which a 54-year-old Hometown man was killed near Phoenix earlier this week.

A similar method of updating stories is used by papers that are unavoidably scooped by the competition because of the time the story broke.

For instance, if a local woman was found shot to death about 7 p.m., the morning paper could include a story about the death in its paper the next morning. But the afternoon paper would not be able to report it until it came out the next afternoon. So it will play a game of leapfrog, trying to leap beyond the information of its morning competitor. And if the morning paper runs a follow-up story the next day, it will try to leap beyond the information run by its afternoon competitor.

The jumping competition might look like this:

The body of a 21-year-old Hometown woman was discovered in an alley behind the South Side Tap Monday night. [first story in the morning paper]

Police today are looking for the boyfriend of a murdered 21-year-old Hometown woman fatally shot Monday to question him about her death. [first story in the afternoon paper]

A 22-year-old Hometown man was arrested Tuesday night and charged with the shotgun shooting of his girlfriend. [second story in the morning paper]

Sometimes papers make the mistake of stretching too far in contriving to find a current-sounding approach, losing sight of the real news.

Localize

Localize your lead whenever possible. Readers are especially interested in learning about what is happening on their home turf. If there is a local angle to the story, try to work it into the lead. It will help attract reader attention.

Don't exaggerate

Make sure the lead does not go beyond the facts of the story. Yes, you want to attract reader attention, but not by making any false claims.

For instance, if you have interviewed five people and gathered their reactions to the election victory of the first woman to become county executive, do not write a lead that says:

Everyone seemed happy today about the election of a woman to the position of county executive.

You have only talked to five people. To say that everyone seemed happy is an exaggeration. Instead you could report that:

Everyone interviewed today applauded the election of a woman to county executive.

Use wrap-up leads when appropriate

Sometimes you may need to write a lead for a story that rounds up information about related incidents with a common theme, such as all the weekend accidents in the area. That type of story is called a round-up or a wrap-up.

Often the kind of lead that will work best for such a story is one that gets at all the incidents but at the same time singles out the most newsworthy bit of information. For instance:

An 81-year-old man died of smoke inhalation in one of three house fires in Earlsville today.

Use quotes sparingly

A quote will occasionally work well as a lead. But do not just use it because it is a quick, easy way to begin.

The quote must get at the aspect you consider the most newsworthy. And it must do it clearly and directly. If it doesn't do the job, try a different approach.

Avoid focusing on what did not happen

Use your lead to emphasize what did, not what didn't happen. Avoid leads such as: "No one was injured in a car–truck accident on Route 41 today."

Keep it tight

Make sure your lead is tight enough. A one-sentence hard news lead made up of more than 35 words is probably difficult to follow. Try solving the problem by dividing the original sentence into two sentences.

But leads with far fewer words can also suffer from not being direct enough. Be careful not to include distracting information that would better be reported later in the story. The exact time that an accident occurred, for instance, is that kind of information. In your lead just report what day the accident occurred or perhaps that it happened in the morning or evening, but do not confuse the readers with the hour of the day.

Similarly, often it is best to save names for later. Many editors will ask you to include in your leads only those names that would be well-known to readers. If the mayor of the city were in an accident, use his or her name. For less prominent individuals more general identification such as "a 16-year-old Hometown youth" is best. Then identify that person by name in the second paragraph.

A large proportion of leads are one-sentence paragraphs, but you can vary from that format. Especially in stories using a feature tone, the best approach may be a paragraph with two or more sentences. For instance, take this Associated Press lead:

Lowy Schultz, glad to be recalled to his job at Caterpillar Tractor Co., packed up his family and returned 1,600 miles from Arizona. Six hours after he punched in, he was laid off again.

The two sentences used in this lead work well to capture the calamity that struck the worker so soon after his return to his old job. The longer, flowing first sentence has a kind of leisurely quality. It suddenly smacks into a short, staccato sentence that describes the end of his high hopes. The pace of the sentences reflects his situation. The two sentences combine to provide the kind of effective opener that a single sentence might have been unable to achieve.

And sometimes even several paragraphs may be needed as a lead to set the mood for a feature story. I thought the feature on the Experimental Aircraft Association's convention and fly-in I wrote as a stringer for *The Milwaukee Journal* required that kind of more leisurely approach.

> In sun-colored biplanes they come. In cherished old warbirds, in tiny experimental home-built planes painstakingly assembled in basements.
>
> In expensive Learjets they come. From air strips on little farms, from major aviation centers, from Australia, Japan, England and every state in the United States—they come. Commercial pilots, aviation designers, doctors, farmers, the man who pedaled the plane across the English Channel, record-holding balloonists, pilot (and singer) John Denver—all are regulars at the annual Experimental Aircraft Association's convention in Oshkosh.
>
> For one week each year, Oshkosh has the busiest airport in the world as it becomes the focus of a sort of pilgrimage dedicated to a celebration of American ingenuity and adventure.

I could have just started that feature with a one-sentence, one-paragraph lead that said:

> When the Experimental Aircraft Association is held in Oshkosh each year, it has the busiest airport in the world.

But that solution to the lead problem did not get at the feeling of the convention I was trying to convey.

In writing the more rambling lead, I knew I was putting together a story for a Sunday paper where space is usually more plentiful and stories longer because readers often tend to read their Sunday papers in a more leisurely way. Such factors must be considered in writing leads. As in everything else, it is important to keep in mind the task before you and adjust your writing accordingly.

Often you may not have the luxury of that additional space. Much of what you will be writing will be hard news stories that have to deliver their information quickly.

In some cases in a hard news story you may decide you can get at that information most effectively by using a main lead and a secondary lead. This solution may be the best bet when two almost equally important bits of news are contained in the story. Include the information about the most important aspect in the first sentence, the other news in the secondary lead. For instance:

> The Belnap City Council voted Monday night to approve a 12% increase in the property tax rate.
>
> It also authorized a reassessment of all residences on the east side of the city.

When you write the rest of the story after completing the lead, provide more information about the main lead first, then continue on and develop the secondary lead.

Check on appropriateness

When you have finished writing the whole story, go back and read the lead carefully to make sure that it is appropriate for the article you have ended up writing. Sometimes a story may take a very different direction than you had originally envisioned. If so, change the beginning accordingly. And make sure that the tone of the lead is appropriate for the tone of the rest of the piece.

Be Critical

Remember—with leads as with everything you write, a certain amount of distance is important. Do not become too closely attached to your words. Stand back from your stories and read them as a reader might, making sure that what you write is clear and interesting. And if it is not—change it.

It is amazing how the passage of time makes that kind of distance and objectivity so much easier. When the rush of deadlines allows, try setting a story aside for a couple of days, then reread it. Rough passages in need of rewriting are likely to jump out at you. See if you can develop that kind of objectivity for paragraphs you have just finished writing.

Rarely does even the finest writer create something that could not be improved upon. And that is especially true for journalists who have to write quickly because of the demands of deadlines.

Even the prestigious *The New York Times*, which is generally agreed to be the best paper in the country, recognizes that its writers make mistakes. It cites problem passages as well as outstanding work in a bulletin it calls *Winners and Sinners*. They will mail copies to you for $25 a year.[1]

Keeping in mind that it is a lot easier to play Monday-morning quarterback than to write a story under the pressures of deadline, let's look at some leads written by stringers and consider how they might be improved. The names of the areas have been changed.

1. The Bethesda School Board met Monday night and approved two part-time positions.

---

[1]To get on the subscription list, write Winners and Sinners, *The New York Times*, Room 1042, 229 W. 43rd St., New York, NY 10036.

REVISED: The Bethesda School Board approved two part-time positions Monday night.

[If the board approved the positions, it necessarily held a meeting. No need to report that the members met. The lead needed tightening.]

2. The Georgetown School District held their school board meeting last night and the resignation of one school board member was the main topic of the agenda.

[—Again, there is no reason to say the board held its meeting. But more information is needed to rewrite this lead effectively. It is an example of a topic lead that does not get at the most newsworthy, significant information that arose about the topic.

—Also the singular possessive pronoun "its" should be used instead of "their" in referring to the board.]

3. When Georgetown City Council met Monday night, a portion of their discussion centered around repairing parts of the five miles of city streets and alleys.

[This lead suffers from a couple of common lead problems. It backs into the information, and it too is a topic lead.]

4. The Winthrop Village Board heard from a Senior Citizen Committee at last night's meeting.

(—Yes, but what did the committee members say?

—Avoid the wording "at last night's meeting." It is not logical to use the possessive form of "night," although the expression is heard frequently.]

5. A special meeting has been called by the Mendota City Council for later this month.

[On what subject?]

6. The board of Supervisors in Fairfax County found very little pressing business at their regular Monday session this week. They approved a contract to purchase in-home family therapy for one or two county families having potential child abuse problems. The contract with Alternate Treatment Associates is not to exceed $5,000.

[—Tighten up the name of the board and say the Fairfax County Board of Supervisors.

—Do not emphasize the fact that there was little pressing business at the meeting. If nothing newsworthy happened, do not write any story at all. But in this case something newsworthy did happen, as the second paragraph indicates.]

7. The cost of shifting to a "single bus run" schedule for Graystown schools will be calculated for school board review.

[Don't use quotation marks for the purpose of setting off words that might not be completely understood by those who are not directly involved. Instead, remove the quote marks and explain the terms.]

8. With an eye toward safety and costs, the York City Council Tuesday night narrowly approved a detour route for the State Street reconstruction project, slated for next summer utilizing the Interstate, despite pleas from merchants to keep State Street open by working on one lane at a time.

    REVISED: The York City Council Tuesday night narrowly approved a detour route for the State Street reconstruction project, despite pleas from merchants to keep State Street open by working on one lane at a time.

    [The original lead was 48 words long. It illustrates that additional words do not necessarily make the sentence clearer, and often, as in this case, they make it harder to follow.]

9. When a public hearing was held in Madison on rattlesnake bounties last spring, only two people testified, but last night the Abbotsford Village Hall was filled to capacity as more than 60 people jammed the room for a public hearing conducted by the State Senate Committee on Agriculture and Rural Affairs. The hearing was on legislation to allow local government to impose a bounty on troubled rattlesnakes.

    [—It's a rough world. Even the poor rattlesnakes are troubled.

    —Watch the emphasis. There's a great local story here, but it's been made to take a back seat to what happened earlier in Madison, the state capital.]

10. In addressing the Nile Falls Area Chamber of Commerce Board of Directors, A. William Pallman said Small Business accounts for 97 percent of all American business, 55 percent of business input and 43 percent of the nation's gross national product.

    [—Here is an example of what happens when you back into a lead by starting with a prepositional phrase. The speaker presented some interesting statistics. Get at them directly.

    —Who is A. William Pallman? In the lead it would be better to refer to him by his title or some other identification that explains his expertise.

    —There is no reason to capitalize Small Business when used in this way.]

11. The Warren Lions Club recently held a contest to design its first club pin.

    [Remember to emphasize the latest development. In this case, that would be the winning entry, which was described later in the story.]

12. Eric R. Larson, 24, of Greensville, and Clifford L. Olson, 27, of Amityville, had initial appearances today in Lincoln Circuit Court before Judge

Louis I. Drecktrah. They are being held in the Lincoln County Jail on probation holds and are unable to meet $5,000 cash bail bonds.

[—Save the names for later. That will make the lead easier to read.

—Of what crime have they been accused? Be careful to work in the most newsworthy information.]

13. Crossing gates were not used last summer and it was remarkable that there were no car–train accidents.

[Let the reader decide if something is remarkable. The writer has to remain neutral.]

14. A court order to paint 50 fire hydrants in Chester is part of the ruling placed by the Wilson County Circuit Court on Clifford Thomas Gomer, 47, of 212 Oak Street, Chester.

[—Again, save the name for later.

—An interesting tidbit gathered from the court records. Get maximum mileage out of it by featurizing your lead. Make sure the tone of the lead is appropriate for the subject. This lead is too straightforward.]

15. Ray Zahn, who was not a candidate for re-election as Bergen town treasurer this spring, looks back on 20 years of treasury work with much interest.

[Place greater emphasis on his years of service and less on the fact that he is not a candidate.]

16. As hunters poured into Dane for the hunting season there was more than one local woman who breathed that well-known sigh of relief. The onslaught of hunters no longer means the long and tiring preparation of food and rooms for hunters.

And here's the ending: Camping vans, motor homes, converted buses and hunting shacks have erased the need for local hospitality in homes, but many women of Dane look back with enjoyable memories and the importance of the income at hunting time during those years during the Great Depression.

[The story ended up going a different direction than the lead suggested. It would have worked better to emphasize the positive aspects of the days past in the lead. A careful rereading of the total story after you finish it will help ensure that the lead and body of the story function as a unit.]

And then there was this delightful example that turned up among the stories I was asked to review:

A bull, apparently bored with the agricultural day proceedings at the 118th annual Lee County fair, decided to explore Emory's nightlife Wednesday.

While most of the animals were content to stay in their stalls for a little prejudging preening, this bull cruised down the street with Emory policemen in hot pursuit in their squad cars.

To begin with, the writer had the news sense to spot this little gem among the more routine goings-on of the county fair. You too may be able to find similar colorful anecdotes like this among your local police reports from time to time.

And the effective writing style used in the lead really makes it stand out as a great little bright—that is, a short, amusing story valued by editors as a welcome change of pace from the often more ponderous news of the day. Without that effective treatment, an editor may have decided the incident was not even worth a story. But with this stylish lead, such a story might even win a coveted front-page spot. It is an example of the kind of fine pieces that can be produced by an effective wedding of style and substance, even by those stringers who are living in areas where there is little of earth-shattering significance happening during the course of the week.

AND NOW THE REST OF THE STORY

When you wrote your lead, you already developed in your mind a construction plan for the whole story. You had to decide on the focus before writing the first sentence. Much of the organizational task is completed with the creation of the lead.

It remains now to assemble the remaining building blocks of information to construct the article, using the design you had in mind when you formed your lead.

The Inverted Pyramid

The basic blueprint used by journalists to create the standard hard news story calls for an inverted-pyramid approach. That is, the most important news comes at the top of the story with increasingly less significant information added later.

One of the main reasons for forming the story in this way is that readers often read only the first few sentences of the article. They do not have enough interest or time to read every last word before moving on to the next article. By giving them the most crucial information right at the top of the story, you are helping them to gather information as efficiently as possible.

Furthermore, editors faced with the pressure of having to edit stories on deadline so they will fit on the page appreciate a piece that can be trimmed quickly and easily. It is a lot easier for them if they can just chop from the bottom of the story instead of from within.

That layout time pressure is changing somewhat these days as new electronic equipment helps editors know how long a story will run in its printed form and how it will fit on the page.

Someday in the future we may find that the recommended blueprint has changed, perhaps in response to changing needs, but for now the generally accepted ideal hard news format is the inverted pyramid. However, realize that it can be a somewhat raggedy-looking inverted pyramid because you have to consider more than just the news value of the building blocks. The story will flow better and be more easily understood if you group related information together, despite its relative news value.

Feature stories will deviate from the inverted-pyramid style. The assumption is that because they generally have a more timeless quality, they don't have to be handled in the rush of deadline. Editors have more time to make any needed cuts and therefore don't have to trim from the bottom.

As a result, endings of features should not just trail away, as is the case with many hard news articles. A feature must conclude in a satisfying kind of way. One frequently used technique is to save an effective quotation or anecdote for the ending of a feature. And as we have seen, feature leads may not fit into the inverted-pyramid design as they often continue for several paragraphs.

Selecting Your Material

No matter whether you are writing a hard news or a feature story, you have to be discriminating in deciding what to use in building your article. Just because· you have spent a lot of time collecting a particular fact does not mean it has to end up in the story. Many may not be included as building blocks because they do not fit right.

They may be the foundation for another story at a later time or you might just have to throw them out altogether. Adding them to a story where they are inappropriate will only detract from the other material. Often it is not until you look over the total product of your research and start writing the story that you can determine what will be needed and what will not.

Your decision as to what needs to be thrown out has to be determined in part by the length of the articles run in the paper for which you are writing. I knew, for instance, that on a weekday it would be very unusual for *The Milwaukee Journal*, for whom I was stringing, to use a story that ran more than about two typewritten pages. Yes, they made an exception the day I reported on a rookie police officer who killed his wife and two children, then committed suicide. But fortunately such incidents do not happen very often.

Feature sections, especially in Sunday papers, tend to include longer articles. But many editors even of such sections don't want stories to run beyond four pages. Check with your editor for your paper's guidelines on length of articles.

Developing the Lead

As you organize your information, your first task in writing the body of the story is to develop further the information in your lead. Let's say your lead reports:

A 19-year-old Abbotsford man was killed Sunday when the motorcycle he was driving on Route 120 ran into a tree.

Identify him immediately in the next paragraph. For instance, "The cyclist, Gerald Mason of 1451 Bilingsford Road, died of head injuries."

Don't forget about your lead and leave it floating up there all by itself. Tell the reader more about the facts introduced in the lead.

Once you have developed the lead, you can proceed with the rest of the inverted pyramid, adding facts in the order of their importance. Thus, the accident story above might read:

A 19-year-old Abbotsford man was killed Sunday when the motorcycle he was driving ran into a tree.

The cyclist, Gerald Mason of 1451 Bilingsford Road, died of head injuries.

Police said the accident occurred about 11:30 p.m. when Mason, who was headed west on Route 120, lost control of his cycle at a curve a quarter mile west of the Dundee Road intersection.

He was taken to Memorial Hospital where he died 2 hours later without regaining consciousness.

In a feature story an effective bridge has to be used between the opener and the main body of the piece. The opener should have special pizazz, just like the opening of a standup comic, if it is to catch the reader's attention, but it must also help direct the reader to the main focus of the story.

Once you have come up with the creative effort needed to make the feature opener work, do not forget about the bridge that is needed to tie it in with the rest of the story. If you do not write an effective bridge, even though the opener may work well as an attention grabber, it will fail to help get at the focus of the story.

The stringer who wrote the following feature (with the location changed) had a great idea for an opener.

There's a billboard along Highway 20 adjacent to Herbert Thompson Preparatory School that says, "Sentry lives." It's lettered with black paint and no matter how many times it's painted over, someone sneaks in at night with a paint-brush and repaints the simple phrase, "Sentry lives."

Sentry High School, operated by the Jesuits, was the largest boarding school in the country for high school students in the mid-sixties. Enrollment peaked in

1964-65 when over 600 boys attended. The school opened as both a high school and college in 1880.

The opening and bridge are a fine way to get at a story, but not this story, which is about the closing of this once-popular school. The bridge does not work in leading us to the body of the story, which focuses on the closing.

Effective Transitions

You must also remember to add bridges throughout the rest of the piece, cementing your blocks of information together with effective transition. Gary Provost (1983) talked about the technique in an article entitled "Rapid Transit," published in *Writer's Yearbook.* "A transition in writing is a word or group of words that moves you from one place to another," he wrote. "The place might be the location of a scene, a spot in time, or an area of discussion. The transition should be quick, smooth, quiet, reliable and logical, and it should bring to itself a minimum of attention. . . . Transitions occur throughout your writing, not just where paragraphs meet. But the gap between paragraphs is a 'danger zone' where you risk losing readers unless you guide them carefully" (pp. 74, 75).

Check each paragraph of your story to see if it proceeds smoothly from the preceding paragraph. If it doesn't, perhaps you need to add effective transition words. If you cannot come up with good words that will bridge the gaps, the fault may be in the organization. A revamping of that organization is in order.

Accuracy

Your building blocks will consist to a large extent of statistics, examples, and opinions from sources. No matter what the type of information, be absolutely sure that your information is accurate. Inaccuracy is the cardinal sin in the newspaper world. A newspaper's credibility is only as good as its weakest writer. An editor is not likely to allow you to continue writing for the paper if your copy is plagued by inaccuracies. Check and double check your facts.

Directness

In assembling the information you are using, limit your building blocks to one basic idea per sentence and no more than three or four sentences per paragraph.

Get at the information directly. For instance, do not include a passage such as the following:

Sen. Wilma Thompson went on to talk about the effects of the proposed tax cuts. She predicted they would be most beneficial to individuals with higher incomes.

Instead report:

Sen. Wilma Thompson predicted the proposed tax cuts would be most beneficial to individuals with higher incomes.

Attribution

Attributing information can present special problems. A writer must first of all decide when it is necessary to attribute something to a particular source. The basic guideline is that unquestionable facts need not—and should not—be attributed. Phoenix is in Arizona, the St. Patrick's Day parade will begin at 2 p.m. No attribution is needed. But, for instance, reporting that proposed tax cuts will be of greatest benefit to wealthier taxpayers is an opinion with which some might well disagree and that must be attributed.

When quoting the words of a source, the writer has to decide whether to use a direct quote (the exact words of the speaker), indicated by quotation marks, or an indirect quotation or paraphrase of the source's words.

Sometimes, let's face it, your decision will be dictated simply by which words you were able to get down exactly in your notes. Because direct quotes should be exact, you will have to paraphrase that information if you do not have it down exactly.

Many papers will make an exception to the rule of using exact words for direct quotes if the wording is ungrammatical. Editors of those papers will expect you to correct the grammatical errors.

Just because you have managed to preserve a source's exact words in your notes does not mean that you should determinedly inject them into your story. Often paraphrasing is better. Few people talk as clearly and precisely as they write, and by rewording their thoughts, you can get across the same idea in a more direct and effective manner. Especially avoid using direct quotes for more routine information.

But if you want to emphasize the opinion of your source, capture his or her emotion or colorfulness of expression, direct quotes are a great way to do it. They can also serve as a nice change of pace from the rest of your story.

Never use direct quotes because you cannot figure out what the speaker meant and are including the exact words so the reader can decide. Either find out what the intended meaning was and reword the thoughts or leave the quote out completely.

Check each direct quote you have included and decide whether it works effectively. If it doesn't, leave it out or paraphrase it.

You do not always have to use a source's full sentence or sentences in quotation marks, although it is generally preferable to do so instead of using fragmentary quotes. However, you can occasionally just quote several words from the sentence, especially if only those words are clearly and concisely worded. But avoid quoting a single, lone word, known as an orphan quote.

Do not keep the reader guessing about who is being quoted. Avoid going beyond one sentence of quoted material before identifying who is speaking. And when you switch from one speaker to another, it is a good idea to identify the speaker before the quote to make it clear that someone else is speaking.

Ordinarily, you can put the attribution at the end of the quote as well as before it. Or you can break the quoted sentence with attribution words—if you make sure that you are adding the attribution at a natural break in the sentence.

Thus, you can handle direct quotes in the following ways:

Smith said, "Despite the enormous progress they've made, it's a legitimate question whether saving the company was ever a realistic hope."

"Despite the enormous progress they've made, it's a legitimate question whether saving the company was ever a realistic hope," Smith said.

"Despite the enormous progress they've made," Smith said, "it's a legitimate question whether saving the company was ever a realistic hope."

It is a good idea to mix up these forms of attribution to help avoid monotony, especially in a speech story, where a large part of the story will consist of quotes of the speaker's words. Be careful that you are attributing throughout in reporting the words of the speaker or it will appear that you, the reporter, are expressing your own thoughts.

You also may want to use some variety in the attribution word you select. You might, for instance, say the speaker "called for" a change in legislation, "charged" that the current legislation discriminates against the poor, or "announced" that he will propose new legislation to correct what he sees as abuses. But if no other attribution word seems to work precisely, do not worry about using "said" over and over again. It is a good, neutral word that is unobtrusive and thus does not call attention to the fact that it is being used frequently.

Be careful to avoid using attribution words with the wrong meaning for the context. For instance, "explain" should be used only when an explanation process is involved. "Stated" and "announced" should be used only for more formal occasions and not just as a substitute for "said."

The word "claim" has a strange way of making whatever is said sound like a lie, as in: "The fire chief claimed firemen investigated the cause of the fire thoroughly." And "reveal" and "disclose" are sometimes misused by over-ambitious reporters who would like to give the impression they have uncovered a great scoop when such is not the case.

In a hard news story, do not report that someone "thinks" or "believes" something. Instead report that someone "said he thinks" or "said he believes" something. The reason? A politician may say he believes the moon is made of green cheese if it will win some votes at election time. You cannot know for sure what he really believes.

Many editors, however, will make exceptions for feature stories where the presumption is that reporters become so familiar with the subject that they can have a better idea of what that source is really thinking. As a result, in a feature story you can, for instance, report that "Smith thinks the race will be close."

Generally, use the natural word order in attributing information. Thus, it should be "Smith said" and not "said Smith."

Do not quote a lifeless object such as a hospital, as in "St. Joseph's Hospital reported today that the number of emergency cases has doubled since last year." Instead, attribute the information to a spokesperson for the hospital.

If someone refuses to be interviewed about a news issue, report that he or she declined to answer questions. If you do not, your readers will wonder why you have been unfair and not given the person a chance to respond.

But be careful you are not suggesting someone is avoiding answering questions when you could not reach that person or there is some other legitimate reason involved. Do not just say someone was "unavailable for comment" when he or she could not be contacted because that wording suggests evasiveness. Instead, report that the individual could not be reached for comment, perhaps adding the reason, such as he or she was out of town or at a meeting.

If the person could not be reached despite repeated messages to return your call, indicate to the reader how many times you called without result. Readers will draw their own conclusions.

Filling the Holes

Watch for holes in your story as you write. Often it is only as you start writing up the information that you realize what you have forgotten to ask. When such holes develop, fill them by calling back your source for further information. Only a lazy, unprofessional reporter allows the holes to remain, sometimes causing the whole story to collapse.

No matter how proficient a writer you are, your story can only be as good as the information you have collected to create it. If you are having trouble putting the story together, perhaps the problem is that you need to do more legwork before you start writing.

The Quest for Perfection

Do not expect to be a perfect writer from the moment you sit down at a typewriter. You may be a great lover of classical music and the mellow sounds of a well-played violin. But the first time you pick up a violin and try to play it, some terribly unpleasant sounds will be produced by that bow. You know how it should sound, but your feeble attempt is a far cry from that sound. Even after 2, 3, even 20 years of practicing you may be dissatisfied with the sounds you are making. The greatest virtuosos are constantly working at improving their art.

So, too, it is with writing. Although you may be an ardent reader and fan of great writing, your own early attempts may be less than you had hoped. Be patient. Practice makes better, although not perfect. Fortunately, there is always room for improvement and writing offers a never-ending challenge.

Watch the works of others and borrow their techniques. The most creative of individuals borrow from the styles of others. There is no point in reinventing the wheel. Many before you have put pen to paper and expressed their thoughts. But in borrowing from their talents, take what feels most comfortable to you.

Keep an eye out for the best of journalistic writing today. *The Wall Street Journal*, with its finely crafted stories honed into shape by skillful editors, is a good place to look. You might also consider subscribing to *The New York Times* to see how the best of American journalists do their thing.

As with many pursuits that require the development of talents, your early effort may result in the almost childlike discovery of the excitement of a new and satisfying experience.

Next come years of trial and error and development of technique. You will be exploring what is possible—what works and what does not and how to accomplish your task as efficiently and effectively as possible.

And finally, once you have mastered the basic techniques of your craft, you can begin to start playing around with your style, bringing your own special individuality to your writing in producing feature stories or other types of pieces for which such style is appropriate.

But remember—developing your writing skills takes a lot of time, effort, and energy. Yes, in some ways writing for a newspaper is glamorous work—you will be rubbing elbows with the famous and assuming a bit of celebrity status in your own right as your byline becomes known. But a lot of hard, grueling hours before a typewriter, not to mention in researching the story, are involved in earning that glamour.

And no doubt, over the long haul, you will find that more rewarding than the glamour is the never-ending challenge involved in being a successful writer.

EFFECTIVE
INTERVIEWING

As a journalist, there are several ways you can gather information in constructing your stories. And those techniques are likely to differ significantly from previous research efforts you have undertaken as a student writing research papers—then, you probably relied heavily on already published material. Because you are now writing news, published research materials such as books, magazines, and encyclopedias on which you had depended so much as a student are of little use to you except as background information.

As a collector of news you may frequently draw upon written information, but rarely is it published material. You might, for instance, use police reports or a consultant's report on recommendations for development of your downtown area. But such written matter makes up only a small part of the information you use for your stories.

Another basis of information you might use in your newspaper research is direct observation. For instance, you could observe and then describe how local firefighters battled a raging department store fire. But it is rare when you will be able to use your own observations in compiling your information. Usually you will have to rely on facts provided by others.

A large proportion of information found in newspaper articles is collected by interviewing sources. As a result, it is of utmost importance that you become an effective interviewer.

Phone Interviews

Much of the interviewing you will be doing will be over the phone. A reporter does not have time to dash out and talk to all of the various sources interviewed during the course of a news day. A considerable amount of the job involves one phone call after another.

At the outset of each phone call, be sure to identify yourself and the paper for which you are reporting. If the source you are trying to reach is unavailable at the moment, leave a message asking that he or she return the call.

Usually it is also a good idea to leave word about the nature of your questions. That will give your sources a chance to collect their thoughts and perhaps compile some information that might be useful when they talk to you later. On rare occasions, when you think catching the individuals off-guard might be helpful in getting forthright answers, do not give them any forewarning as to your line of questioning.

Rounding up information by phone instead of interviewing someone in person can save a lot of time. And every minute you save in collecting information can be used in working on other stories and providing the kind of thorough coverage your editor needs. But there are times when it is essential to interview someone face to face. For instance, if you are writing a personality profile about someone, you have to get to know his or her environment, mannerisms, style of dress, and total personality. You need to meet your subjects, to watch them talk.

Preparing for Face-to-Face Interviews

To set up face-to-face interviews, contact your sources in advance and line up a time when it would be convenient for them to talk to you.

Usually the best way to handle the arrangements is just to call the person and schedule a time and place. There are occasions, however, when you may find you will be making the arrangements via written communication. For instance, if part of your responsibility includes covering a prison in your area, you will find you cannot just call the prisoners and arrange an interview. You may have to write them and request an interview, then arrange with the authorities to get into the prison.

It is almost always best to approach the person directly, but sometimes you will need to make arrangements through a third party. For instance, if your local university is bringing in a famous guest speaker, your best bet might be to check with the individuals involved in hosting the celebrity while on campus or with the agency that lines up his or her speaking engagements.

There are times, however, when such people may be overprotective of the celebrity, and you are stymied in your attempt to schedule an interview. You may have greater success if you get directly to the person you hope to interview.

Take the time when actress Kathryn Crosby, wife of the late Bing Crosby, came to my area of Wisconsin to perform in a show. *The Milwaukee Journal* drama writer had tried unsuccessfully in advance of her arrival to secure an interview. Because he could not line up an interview, he decided not to drive the almost 2 hours each way to cover the performance, and I was assigned the job as the *Journal* stringer for the area.

When I got there, I decided to make one last attempt for an interview for our paper, and sure enough, Mrs. Crosby, who at one time had herself been a newspaper writer, graciously agreed to talk to me after the grueling two-person show.

When you are trying to line up an interview, tell your intended subject what you want to talk about as well as who you are and with whom you are affiliated. If you plan to try to sell the resulting piece to more than one newspaper or to a magazine as well as your newspaper, be sure to mention that. For instance, when I interviewed the president of the U.S. Amateur Tug-of-War Association for a story on the international tug-of-war competition in Oshkosh, Wisconsin, which ended up on the front page of *The Milwaukee Journal*, I asked that source if it would be all right if I also used the information in a possible magazine article. Wanting to spread the word about the growth of the pulling competition as a legitimate sport, he readily agreed. His quotes are included in an article I sold to *Sports Parade* magazine. It would not be fair for sources to suddenly see themselves quoted in publications without such forewarning.

Former Moral Majority leader Jerry Falwell's reaction is an example of how sources might respond when they see information they provided show up in a publication for which they did not realize they were being interviewed. In his case, that publication was *Penthouse* magazine and the religious leader's response was to contact his lawyer.

Also give your subjects an idea of how long the interview will last. If you plan to write a profile, ask them to set aside at least an hour of time.

If you need to write an extensive in-depth description of the subject, you may have to spend a lot more time—sometimes even following him or her around for days. That is how the famous *Playboy* interviews, a regular feature in the men's magazine, are often conducted. Take, for instance, its revealing interview with singer Paul McCartney and his wife, Linda. That interview was conducted by free lancer Joan Goodman over a period of about 6 months.

To find out more about your profile subjects, you also need to talk to others about them. Your subjects are not likely to tell you, for instance, that money is their main motivation in life and that they cheated their friends to gain their goals. But on the other hand, neither are they likely to tell you about their virtues. Because one of those virtues may well be modesty, you may never learn about the others without checking with acquaintances. Those talks with people who know the subject should be held before the interview with the person to be written about. That allows you to draw upon comments made by others in questioning the interviewee.

Having done your homework thoroughly in advance of the interview can also help you establish better rapport with your subject and put you in tighter control of the interview. Your interviewee will appreciate being interviewed by someone who is well-versed in the subject and may welcome a chance to move quickly beyond the basic background information and converse with someone who has that kind of knowledge. Also, your backgrounding will help prevent you from getting deceived by someone who has something to hide and may try to lead you astray.

Dealing With Refusals to Talk

Occasionally you will run across individuals who will refuse to talk to you, especially if they know you are planning to ask tough questions. How do you deal with this situation?

Sometimes it will work to remind the individuals of their public responsibility. If they are government employees, suggest that it is part of their duty to the public they serve to answer the questions you hope to pose.

And for both those in the private and the public sectors, it may be effective to argue that their thoughts, because of their special expertise, would be of great help to readers.

Some professionals, like doctors, have over the years been reluctant to talk to the press because of the notion that the kind of publicity that results is somehow unprofessional. Especially in such cases it may help to point out the need the public has to hear from them.

Here is an example of a physician who learned that lesson as a result of what happened when he declined to talk to a reporter. One of his colleagues on the hospital staff was attempting to win permission to use a midwife at the hospital and described his thoughts to a newspaper reporter. In attempting to get the other side of the story, the reporter dutifully called the first-mentioned physician, who opposed the use of a midwife because he strongly believed health risks were involved. But he declined to talk to the reporter, and only his colleague's position ended up in the story. No doubt the remembrance of this one-sided account will make him think twice about questions from the press in the future.

Sometimes when an individual declines to be interviewed, you may want to try to get a comment from someone else in the same organization. Often, surprisingly, the person at the top may be the easiest to reach. That top individual is likely to be in a position of commenting without incurring repercussions from others in the organization and thus can be less defensive and more open. As a result, it is often a good idea to ask the person at the top for a comment.

Some organizations, you will find, have designated only one person to answer questions from the outside. Others in the organization have been told not to talk to the press. Often that spokesperson is a hired public relations specialist who is an expert at putting his or her organization in the best possible light.

The problem is that that individual may not have the expertise to answer the kinds of questions you need to ask. The PR representative may offer to go to the resident expert for a response and then report back to you, but that situation, in which you are unable to question the expert directly, can be a very ineffective way of conducting an interview.

Working as a correspondent for some time in the same area and developing a collection of trusted sources can be of great help when the organizational structure prevents you from getting through to the right employee. Often you come to know of individuals who might be opposed to the company line and would like to get their point across. You may have to contact them at home rather than at work and promise them anonymity, but by doing so you may get a full accounting of what is going on.

If all else fails and you are unable to elicit a comment to a question crying out for a response, inform the subject you had hoped to interview that you will have to report that he or she declined to comment. That potential source will no doubt understand the negative connotation such refusal would suggest to the reader. The result may be a change of heart and a decision to be interviewed.

Dressing for the Part

For interviews conducted in person, give some thought to how you dress. You will feel very uncomfortable and perhaps be less likely to elicit open answers to your questions if you go down to the docks and interview a dock worker in your three-piece suit. On the other hand, don't go into a formal office setting in your blue jeans.

When I was working at columnist Jack Anderson's office, my generally casually dressed male colleagues had a community sports jacket in the office that they donned when they had to go out to talk to a congressman or some similar personage. The time would come when I wished that community jacket fit me. Attired in a casual pair of slacks one morning, I suddenly found out that the president had called a press conference and I was to attend. Quickly I went out and invested in a dress at a nearby shop, then headed to the White House.

It is not that the security people at the gate would have prevented me from entering the White House in slacks. But I would have felt very uncomfortable.

When you are in a position of interviewing someone, it is important to feel as comfortable and secure as possible. Your attitude can play a large role in the kind of response you get.

Your approach can also affect the way interviewees respond to your questions. You can communicate the kind of response you might personally view most favorably through the tone of your voice, your gestures, and the way you phrase a question. To discourage sources from just giving you the answer they guess you think is the right one, try to ask the questions in as neutral a manner as possible.

Sometimes you might deliberately alter the tone of your voice to help control an interview. For instance, in cases where you question the veracity of what a source is saying, you might try to indicate that to the individual through the tone of your voice. You want that interviewee to know you are wise to the fibs.

But there are some factors in your image and thus the response you may get to your questions that you are unable to change. Sex is one such given. Research findings indicate that male interviewers obtain fewer responses than females and that they receive the fewest responses from other males.

Age of the interviewer can also have an effect. Research indicates that young people tend to give more answers indicating rejection of authority figures when questioned by an interviewer who is also young. And it has been found that Black respondents feel a distance between themselves and White interviewers and thus tend to suppress answers. In some cases, editors may need to be conscious of these differences in assigning reporters to stories.

Questioning

Even after you have spent years interviewing people, you will find you need to write down intended questions in advance of the session. Do not rely on your memory and the ability to come up with good questions on the spur of the moment. Otherwise, after the interview is over, you may find there are many things you have neglected to ask.

Writing down the questions helps you to zero in on the focus the interview is apt to take. It is a good idea to come up with at least 15 questions. If you list them in a logical order and place the subject's responses after them, it will expedite your task of writing a good, well-organized story.

Be careful not to be too confined by your prepared questions. Listen carefully to your source's responses and be ready to ask additional questions based on what the person is telling you. Often you will get off into territory you had never considered when you drew up the questions. Be a good listener—and be flexible.

Although they can sometimes be unpleasant, be prepared to ask negative questions, if appropriate. It is all part of the job. You are not there trying to impress people and make them like you. You are there to get the story.

But hold up on those negative questions until you have eased into the interview with other questions. One reason for this approach is that the source may decide to terminate the interview rather than respond to such questions. If you have already found out a lot of other information, the interview will not be a total loss. Another reason is you want the source to realize that you are fair and that the negative questions are just part of the total questions you are asking. Your earlier conversation will help you establish that.

Develop a rapport with your subjects and make them feel at ease. If you have ever been interviewed, you know how frightening it can be. You are really at the mercy of your interviewer. The writer can pick what information to include and emphasize, thereby determining in how sympathetic a light you are presented to the world. That is scary.

To be a good interviewer, you have to be a bit of an amateur psychologist. Different kinds of individuals have to be worked with differently. The mayor who is used to dealing with the press on a regular basis needs to be approached in a very different way than the elderly woman with 79 cats who has never been questioned by an interviewer before. She is likely to be more afraid, more hesitant in responding to questions and will need more reassurance.

These kinds of differences should be considered in deciding whether to use a tape recorder to capture an interview. The recorder may inhibit the cat lover but not the more seasoned pro. If the recorder is likely to be a hindrance, leave it at home. But no matter who the subject is, request permission before using a tape recorder.

Similarly, a notebook can be very inhibiting. You might want to keep your notebook tucked away at the outset of the conversation while you engage in some opening chatter to relax your subject.

Be on the lookout for icebreakers. Check the room around you. Is there a prized fish hanging on the wall? Some comments on fishing might be a good starter.

I once had a student who told me he kept in mind this suggestion I had made to his class when he researched what turned out to be an award-winning story on a local drug-related homicide. To break the ice, he said, he lit up a joint with one of his sources, and the source proceeded to reveal a lot of the mysteries in the case. Not exactly what I had in mind when I gave the class that suggestion, and I do not recommend it. But do try to put your subjects at ease.

Be careful how you respond to their responses. Remember that your role is to be an objective reporter. Do not take stands, either gushing support of or lashing out objections to your source's thoughts. Generally it is a good idea not to respond at all except with further questions.

But some people may need a bit more support than that. Especially if you are conducting an interview over the phone, you may have to provide some feedback from time to time. Let the individual know you are still on the other end of the line and still paying attention.

Ask specific questions that will elicit all the particulars you need, but also use good open-ended questions that will give them a chance to state opinions and express their emotions. Often those open-ended questions will provide some of the best quotes. But avoid the kind of inane questions sometimes heard from local television reporters. Standing next to the charred ruins of her home, the hapless owner is asked, "How do you feel about the fire?"

To detect when the truth is being stretched, watch out for inconsistencies in what is being said. And draw upon the information you gathered from others in preparing for the interview.

Be careful, however, not to be too suspicious when sources say they cannot remember a certain fact, even if they have remembered many other things that took place during the same period of time. People have selective recall. For instance, many individuals may have a hard time remembering the date when something happened.

Be careful to get down some good exact quotes, especially if you are preparing a personality profile. A tape recorder will help ensure that you have done that, but going back and listening to the interview for a second time to capture quotes from the tape can be a time-consuming process. You can expedite your task if you can develop a system of writing down quotes carefully during the interview.

In addition to taking careful notes of what is said, also record details about what you see when gathering information for a personality profile. What kind of pictures adorn the walls, what magazines are lying around, what is the subject wearing, what gestures does he or she use while talking? These kinds of tidbits can add a very human touch to a profile.

Maintaining Control

Remember that you are not the focus of the interview. Do not monopolize the conversation. Keep the spotlight on the subject. But at the same time, do not let yourself be shoved around and manipulated. You have to be in control of the interview at all times.

If the source starts going off on an irrelevant tangent, courteously direct the conversation back to the subject at hand. If you fall behind in taking notes, ask the source to pause for a moment while you write down something you would like to include. If a statement is made that is unclear or needs further development, ask your subject to elaborate. You are the expert on what will make worthwhile reading. Play editor as you conduct the interview and keep it on course to ensure that you get the appropriate material.

Maintaining control of the interview is also important because you must try not to impose on the subject's time any more than is necessary. People worthy of an interview tend to be very busy individuals. Their time is valuable.

After Your Questioning

Before concluding an interview, give your subject a chance to add to what has been said or to emphasize or restate points already made. You may be surprised. Some of the material added may be the most important information you have gathered and something you had no way of knowing and asking about. And because the source has had a chance to rethink ideas during the course of the interview, ideas already alluded to may be restated in a much clearer, more powerful manner. Some of your best quotes may come out of this concluding portion of your interview.

Sometimes at this stage of the game you may have sources ask if they can read the story before it is published. Many papers have rules against such a reading—and for good reason. Sources may want to rewrite the piece allowing them to appear in the best possible light, and that is no way to run a newspaper. Stories must be written by the reporter, not the source. And even if a source does not ask to rewrite passages, editors do not want reporters to be pressured into writing only positive things because of the subtle pressure they feel knowing the interviewee will read it in advance. Generally, it is best to courteously refuse to grant such a request.

But you might want to make an exception for a highly technical story that you would like an expert source to read in advance of publication to ensure you have not made any errors. Perhaps, for instance, the nuclear power plant in your area has been temporarily shut down for repairs. You might want your source to check over your description of the kind of repairs being made.

Before you bid farewell to your interview subject, think carefully about what are likely to be the most usable pieces of information you have accumulated. If you have any doubts about that information, double check it with your source.

If you are planning on writing something negative about someone, be careful you have given that person a chance to respond to all aspects of the accusations made against him or her. Each individual charge should have a response.

Avoiding Misunderstandings

Be careful you have not erred in your perception of what has been said. In their book *All The President's Men,* Bob Woodward and Carl Bernstein described when they made that kind of mistake in their investigation of the Watergate scandal.

They told how they mistakenly thought their source, Hugh Sloan, said he had testified about certain information about White House Chief of Staff H. R. Haldeman during secret grand jury testimony. Actually, although the damaging facts about Haldeman appear to have been true, Sloan was not questioned on that subject during the grand jury proceedings. Their paper, *The Washington Post*, had been sticking its neck way out on the Watergate allegations, and that misinformation seriously damaged its credibility for a while.

Listen carefully and make sure you understand thoroughly what your source is attempting to convey. In the end, the key to a good interview is you. As Ken Metzler (1989) wrote in his book *Creative Interviewing*, "Successful interviewers . . . come to listen and understand, not to accuse and judge" (p. 12).

Be a good listener and do not stand in judgment. Empathize and struggle to understand what your subject is telling you. Exercise your curiosity. And revel in the fascinating traits and diversity of humankind.

WORKING ON DEADLINE

Newspapers are just that—papers that report on what is news. Keeping abreast of what is going on at home and abroad and informing readers about it immediately can be quite a challenge. Tomorrow's history has to be written quickly in the mad rush of today. Antacid pills are apt to be a common sight around a newspaper office.

A 1985 British study of stress conducted by researchers at Manchester University found that journalism tied for third place among 150 occupations studied to determine the amount of stress they generate. Miners, with an 8.3 rating, came in first followed by policemen with 7.7 points. Journalists, with 7.5, tied with pilots, prison officers, and construction workers. Librarians, with 2.0, were found to have to endure the least amount of stress.

But some people thrive on deadline pressure. The dash to complete a story may be as crucial to get a reporter's day off and rolling as the next person's morning cup of coffee. Keeping one's wits and writing an effective story under the gun can be a real rush. It is not unlike the exhilaration the soldier gets on the field of battle and a police officer gets stalking a murderer. The task itself can be an unpleasant one, but the test under fire has its satisfactions.

Deadline Productivity

It is amazing to see the amount and quality of work that can be produced in a short amount of time. Like other outsiders, you might well have been surprised when you first saw the size of the staff at the office of the newspaper for which you are working. How can so few turn out so much copy? Somehow, when the need arises, professional journalists seem to be up to the challenge.

You will probably find that after some practice you too are able to be surprisingly productive on deadline. The need is there. And it is as if you go on automatic pilot to get the work done.

Think how much more you could accomplish if you were operating under a constant round of deadlines. Good free-lance writers will try to create that kind of sense of deadline pressure to keep themselves moving on their work. By the end of the day, they tell themselves, they must have written perhaps 10 pages or 3,000 words. You might want to try a similar system of goals to motivate yourself and enhance your productivity.

As a newspaper correspondent, it is crucial that you be conscious of the deadlines of the paper or papers for which you are stringing. What day of the week does a weekly go to press? What is the deadline time faced by your editor? An afternoon daily paper might have a deadline of about noon. A morning paper might not go to press until 10 p.m. Check with your editor for the times.

Because many of you are stringing for more than one paper, you will be facing deadlines at various times of the day. And even if you are working for just one paper, you may be faced with a number of deadlines during the day. Some papers have different editions for various areas they serve, each with its own deadline.

And even within the same edition, varying deadlines have been set for the different pages of the paper. Typically the pages with the most advertising are scheduled for earlier deadlines. Wide open pages free of ads are left available for later breaking stories. Special sections, such as lifestyles, often have earlier deadlines because they are not as dependent on late-breaking stories as are the hard news sections.

Each page has a time assigned as to when it must be ready for the stories to be pasted down. And the production employees have a scheduled time when the pastedowns have to be completed. That schedule must be carefully adhered to, even if it is hours from the time when the total paper will go to press, or the pages would bunch up and the final deadline could not be met. To attain that deadline goal, all have to do their part. If only one person fouls up, the paper can come out late, and disgruntled readers all around the area have to wait to get the news. And that responsibility for timely handling of stories is shared by you as a stringer.

As a result, it is important to organize and plan ahead. If possible, start compiling your information way in advance of your deadline. Let your editor know what you have coming so it can be considered when space is being set aside for various stories.

Often you will need to work on more than one story at a time because you have to wait till a source gets back to you before finishing the first story you have embarked on. In the meantime, compile information on whatever else you have to work on. Juggling and organizing information from several stories at once is a challenge but gets easier with practice.

Sometimes it will be impossible to gather the information until a few minutes before deadline. Perhaps, for instance, you are covering a meeting and an important vote is not taken until minutes before your deadline. Occasionally the timing may prevent you from having enough time to write the story before calling your office and dictating it. Instead, you will just have to collect your thoughts and dictate it without the assistance of anything but the notes you took as the meeting progressed.

In such cases, try to write as much as possible at the same time you are covering the meeting. Add on the final vote or other newsworthy elements you accumulate at the last minute to what you did have a chance to get down in written form. To help you report the most newsworthy points in your notes quickly, put asterisks or some other attention-getting symbols alongside that information.

Portable electronic typewriters and computers can be of great value if you are working on a story on deadline. Some are so small you can stick them in a briefcase and take them along to the event you are covering. With appropriate computer equipment you can transmit your copy directly to another computer at the newspaper office. Just type it up and transmit it via a telephone.

Because they are so quiet to operate, you can type while a meeting or other proceeding is going on and be ready to dictate your typewritten copy before the proceeding has ended. The only drawback I have found with my electronic equipment is that people are so curious about it that my rush for deadline is interrupted by onlookers watching me type and asking questions about what I am doing.

Advance Material

In some situations when you know you will be facing a tight deadline, you might want to write up background information for the news story and dictate it to your paper ahead of time. Then later add to the story the latest developments unavailable until deadline. Usually those late-breaking facts will end up in the lead and the background information will be reported later in the story. Some papers refer to such information prepared in advance as "A copy" or "A matter." It should be written in such a way that no matter what develops and ends up in the lead, the advance information can be run as is without having to make time-consuming changes.

In addition to preparing such background information, you may be asked to write a variety of leads that would cover the various possibilities of what may actually happen. When the results are known, the appropriate lead can be selected and quickly added to the story. For instance, take the way I was assigned to cover the Miss Wisconsin pageant for *The Milwaukee Journal*.

The winning contestant is not named until about 10 p.m. on Saturday, right on deadline for one of the *Journal's* Sunday editions. As a result, my editor asked me to write a number of leads, each heralding the crowning of a different contender. I picked the four competitors I thought had the best chance and wrote a lead for each. Fortunately, one of them was chosen Miss Wisconsin, and the editor, watching the pageant on television back in the newspaper office, quickly turned to that lead and added it to the other background I had dictated earlier.

Sometimes when news events you would ordinarily cover using police or fire officials' reports are happening on deadline, you may have to dash to the scene and try to cover them there instead of relying on the reports. The authorities may still be at the scene and will not have a chance to return to their office and write up their reports by the time your deadline arrives.

Take what happened on an otherwise quiet and lazy Good Friday, for instance. I was sprawled out on the couch when suddenly I got a call from the state desk of *The Milwaukee Journal.* They had heard that several people had been murdered but were unable to get information from the authorities.

We were right on deadline. I called the local police to see what I could find out. All I was able to learn was there had been an incident in a large subdivision on the western side of town. Giving up on getting any more information by phone, I jumped into my car and raced off to that distressingly large subdivision. Luckily I encountered a child on a bicycle who was able to direct me to the scene of the murder. The police were still there investigating but had not yet had a chance to file a report. It turned out that a rookie police officer had killed his wife and two children, then committed suicide. We were unable to get the identities of the individuals for that edition of the paper but were able to get in some basic information.

Your Editor's Schedule

As a stringer working away from the newspaper office, it is easy to forget about the pressure of deadlines hanging over the newsroom. There it is hard to forget. The pace quickens and the pressure mounts as the deadline looms closer. Remember the pressures of those colleagues and work to make their job as easy and effective as possible by getting in stories way before deadline when you can.

And remember those deadline pressures when getting in touch with your editor for various reasons. Save less pressing questions for times when the editors are out from under their deadlines. If you are not sure whether they have finished up their deadline tasks, ask if they have and offer to call back later if they have not. Your concern will be appreciated, and your questions can be responded to more thoroughly when time pressures and worries about soon-to-be published stories do not interfere with the attention your editor can devote to you.

C H A P T E R ■ 8

COVERING SPEECHES

Sometimes you may be asked to cover speeches. That assignment to report on someone's prepared remarks is generally easier than writing a story based on comments from an interview. In most cases, your story is well laid out for you by the speaker, who has given much forethought to the points he or she would like to make. And it is usually not a time-consuming assignment because rarely do speeches last for much more than an hour.

Before going to the event, make sure you have any needed background on the speaker. Hang on to advance publicity you have been sent about the speech. Often that will include helpful biographical information. Sometimes you may need to do further research on the speaker.

At times your job may be made easier by an advance text. Some speakers write down what they plan to say and are willing to make copies of that text available to the press. Check ahead of time to see if such copies are available.

Sit right up front to ensure that you can hear the speaker's words clearly and to be able to get to the individual right after the speech if you have any questions.

If you are lucky enough to have a prepared version of the speech to use, be sure to watch it closely as the speaker delivers his or her remarks. Often the speaker will deviate from the prepared text, leaving out portions, adding others, and sometimes changing the remarks. Follow the text word by word and make the changes to sections you expect to quote. Underline quotable sections.

If you do not have a prepared text, you will have to rely on your own note taking for good direct quotes. Be on the alert for such statements. Again, as with interviews, you may want to take a tape recorder to record the comments. Whether or not you use a recorder, be sure you get down some good quotes word for word. Do not rely solely on your recorder. For some reason it may not record properly and you are left without a story.

If something sounds very quotable, keep it firmly in mind and write it down as quickly as possible, letting other statements go by without recording them as you take a moment to get down all the words of the quotable statement. With practice, you will start to develop an instinct for knowing what will make a good quote. Before you develop that kind of sense, err on the side of taking too many notes. It is a lot better not to use all of the material in your notes than suddenly to realize you do not have enough copy to do justice to the speech.

Lead

Your first challenge in writing up the story, of course, will be the lead. One of your decisions will involve how to refer to the speaker in the lead. Do not just use the name in the lead if the reader will not know who it is. If it is not a familiar name, identify the speaker in some other way, for instance, as the president of the Mercersville Chamber of Commerce.

In deciding whether the name would be familiar to your readers, do not just make a judgment based on whether you know the name. The name should be recognizable to readers in general, including those of all ages.

The variation in name recognition depending on age was brought home to me one time when I was explaining to students in my journalism class how to handle identification in the lead. I was describing to them how I used the name of 1960s political activist Jerry Rubin in a story I was writing for *The Milwaukee Journal*. Who is Jerry Rubin, they wondered. For someone like myself who had gone to college in the 1960s, it was a household name, but not for those college students of the 1980s.

Do not write topic or label leads. Your emphasis in the lead should be on the most newsworthy information presented by the speaker. Look for something specific said about a topic and not just a general topic discussed. For instance, report:

> The president of the Mercersville Chamber of Commerce predicted Monday that new industry will add close to 1,000 new jobs to the area during the upcoming year.
>
> DON'T REPORT: The president of the Mercersville Chamber of Commerce talked Monday about the effect of new industry in the area.

Double check your lead to make sure that the information you are reporting is not something the reader might already have known by reading an advance story announcing the speech. If so, your problem probably is that you have written a topic lead.

On rare occasions a direct quote will work well in the lead. But it is unusual that exactly the right information for the lead is expressed in such a quotable form.

In selecting the main focus for the lead, often you will be drawing on the speaker's main point, but sometimes because of its news value, a more casual remark may be the focus for your lead. For instance, the governor may deliver a speech on the state's attempts to lure industry to the state and to keep existing industry. It is the same theme that he has been repeating in recent weeks in speeches throughout the state, and his thoughts have received considerable news coverage.

After once again delivering remarks on the subject, he is asked whether he plans to seek re-election or make a bid for the U.S. Senate seat that will be up for grabs. His response that he plans to seek the Senate seat would under these circumstances make a better lead, even though most of his remarks were delivered on the business climate. That information on luring businesses contained nothing that had not been reported before, whereas this was the first occasion when he had admitted to his Senate ambitions.

Timeliness, of course, has to be considered in determining what to emphasize. If a top State Department official whose special field is Latin America comes to speak at the local college on a day when concern has been raised about Soviet supplying of weapons to Nicaragua, the official's comments on that situation will probably be your lead.

In some cases the lead may emphasize the reaction to the speech. When Ronald Reagan was campaigning in Oshkosh, Wisconsin, in his first bid for the presidency, a heckler threw an egg at him. That egg-throwing was the main focus on national network news, not the remarks made during the course of his speech.

The second paragraph often explains the occasion of the speech and/or provides a bit of biographical background on the speaker. You do not want to weigh your story down with excessive biographical facts because your emphasis should be on what new was said. But you do need to provide enough background on the speaker to enable the reader to judge the credibility and expertise of the person speaking.

Organizing the Rest of the Story

The rest of the story will to a large extent be a weaving together of direct and indirect quotes. First the lead needs to be developed. Then other points should be taken up in order of importance.

How do you know which words might be especially effective as direct quotes?

Be on the lookout for statements representing a strong point of view, especially if related to a newsworthy or controversial matter. And look for unusually worded statements with colorful language.

Do not use direct quotes to report routine matters or to present information that could be stated more concisely and clearly by paraphrasing.

Do not just report on a speech in the same chronological order in which it is delivered. Instead, report the most newsworthy information first, no matter when it was mentioned by the speaker. Often a speaker will start out with a light anecdote, trying to warm up the audience and capture their attention, before moving on to more significant points, so you are not likely to find the lead of your story at the outset of the speech. And many good speakers save the ending of their speech for an effective conclusion that might be mined for lead possibilities.

Report on related points together even if the speaker mentions them at various times during the speech. And do not use the speaker's transitional words suggesting the order of the speech such as "in conclusion" or "moving on to." They do not have any news value.

Often a question-and-answer session follows a speech. You need not report remarks made by the speaker during that session separately from the rest of the comments. If a point made during the formal speech is elaborated on in response to a question, report information from both times together in one place in the story. If the most newsworthy information comes out in response to a question, feel free to use that for your lead.

Focus on the response rather than the question. For instance, do not report: "In response to a question about his position on weapons in space, Sen. Carl Hamilton said he is opposed to development of space weapons."

Instead, simply report: "Sen. Carl Hamilton opposed the development of space weapons."

There may be occasional times, however, when you will want to repeat the question asked to get across to the reader that the speaker was forced by a question to comment on an issue. This happens only rarely, and you will have to use your judgment in deciding when it is necessary.

Attribution

Remember that you have to attribute throughout or it will appear that it is you, the reporter, rather than the speaker who is uttering the thoughts.

Because you have to attribute almost every sentence, a speech story can present one of the greatest attribution problems. It will require a skillful blending of direct quotes and paraphrasing. Avoid a monotonous parade of sentences beginning with "he said" by varying the sentence structure. Sometimes place the attribution at the end of the sentence and other times amid it to get some variety.

Think about the points the speaker is trying to get across and use good substitutes for "said" when appropriate. Not only will they give you more variety but they will help the reader more easily understand what the speaker is saying. For instance, use words like "charged," "criticized," or "opposed" to suggest the speaker's negative comments on a subject. Use words like "supported," "applauded," and "vouched for" to suggest a positive statement.

Sometimes you can hang a number of comments on one verb of attribution. For instance, you might report that "she gave this account" or "she made these points" and follow that attribution with a number of sentences about the speaker's remarks without need for further attribution.

You can also string together several sentences of direct quotes without more than one attribution. But be careful that you are not using too long a passage of direct quotes. Usually some of that long quotation could be better expressed by paraphrasing. Furthermore, such a long passage of quoted matter becomes tedious and tends to bog down your story.

Negative Remarks

Occasionally you will need to get a response to a speaker's critical remarks about someone from the target of those comments. If, for instance, the speaker has questioned the fairness of the layoff procedures of the largest employer in the city, give a representative of that company a chance to explain the procedures.

In other cases your editor may not want you to use some of the speaker's remarks at all because of the danger that they might be libelous. If, for example, the speaker charges that the president of a local bank has embezzled $40,000 in funds and there is no substantiation of such an alleged crime and no charges placed, do not use the remark. Instead, file it away and check on it later.

False or Incoherent Statements

If the speaker states something that you know to be false, do not report it as if it were factual. Remember that you are in the business of reporting what is true, not just accurately reporting whatever someone says, whether it is truthful or not.

How you handle the statement will depend on the situation. If an incumbent running for office talks about the millions of additional dollars his administration has spent to help needy families and you have information that actually there had been a cutback in funds during his administration, report his statement and the actual facts with the source for those facts, letting the reader see the falsehood of what the speaker is saying.

In some cases, however, it will serve no purpose to report the inaccurate information of a speaker. Perhaps he or she has just misspoken or the subject is not significant enough to devote space to pointing out the error. If that is the case, just do not report that remark at all.

What do you do if a speaker babbles on idiotically and does not really say anything? Perhaps he or she is drunk or just plain incoherent out of ignorance. In any case, the speech does not really contain anything of significant value.

If that happens, check with your editor to see how you should handle it. In most cases you will probably be told to forget about the speech and not file a story at all. Many papers will pay you for your time and effort in covering the speech even if no story results. But in some cases, especially a campaign speech, your editor may want you to file a story on the speech, no matter how disjointed it is. Such a story on a campaigning candidate will help readers judge the person who is seeking their vote.

Try to make the tone of your stories fit the tone of the speeches you cover. Covering a humorous speech can be a special challenge. Attempt to give your story the same kind of breezy style that the speech had. Strive to get a lot of good humorous direct quotations into your story to illustrate the speaker's wit.

Other Background

Sometimes the remuneration given to a speaker is newsworthy. Some of the villains of the Watergate scandal have practically made a career out of public speaking. Critics have questioned whether they should reap such large rewards from their speeches, and the amount they are paid is certainly newsworthy. In other cases, the public might well be curious about how much the likes of Henry Kissinger, Jack Anderson, and other such public figures who frequently speak to large audiences are paid. Report their fees.

Also report on who is sponsoring the speech. The size of the audience is also often relevant to mention. If tickets were sold, see how many were purchased. If not, try to estimate the size of the crowd. The easiest way to do so may be to find out how many the hall holds, then estimate what percent of the seats are filled and make your computation. Or you can count how many are sitting in a row or section, then multiply that number by the number of rows or sections in the hall.

In some cases you will need to indicate the reaction of the audience. You may, for instance, have seen reports of the president's State of the Union address that included how often the president was interrupted by applause. The figure helps describe the audience's reactions. Similarly, you might have occasion to report that a speech was received with a standing ovation or was interrupted by hecklers.

Often you may find yourself in the position of covering a panel of speakers. Such a story can be very difficult to organize. Usually it works best to organize it by issue rather than by speaker. Group together what the various panelists had to say on a certain aspect. Do not feel as if you have to give equal space to each panelist. Some may make many more newsworthy comments than others.

Some of the more significant speeches and panel presentations may take place at conferences of newsworthy organizations. If an important conference is being held in your area, get a copy of the agenda and look it over carefully. Especially take note of who the keynote speaker is. That may well be the best part of the conference to cover. Good conference planners often schedule a heavy hitter toward the beginning of the convention to make sure participants arrive on time and to attract their interest.

Do Not Jump the Gun

Never publish the account of a speech until you know for sure that it was actually delivered, even if you have a full copy of the text prepared in advance. You never know when a speaker will become ill, have car problems, or for some other reason be unable to show. Your paper will look very foolish reporting on a speech that never took place.

Suppose you receive an advance text of a speech to be delivered at 2 p.m. It contains highly significant information, but your deadline is noon. How do you handle the situation? The best solution is to go ahead and publish the planned remarks but label them as comments that were prepared for delivery. In that way you are not going to get beaten to the story by your competitors from other media, but neither are you going to have a story reporting that remarks were delivered today when the speaker did not show.

Advance Stories

You may sometimes have to write advance stories notifying the community about upcoming speeches readers may want to go hear. The identification of the speaker and the topic will usually be in the lead. Also somewhere in the story include the date and time of day and the location of the speech. You will also need to provide some biographical information on the speaker.

You may be pleasantly surprised how often fascinating celebrities come to your area to give a presentation. Your job as a stringer will give you an excuse to meet them.

MEETINGS

Like many stringers, you may find meeting coverage will make up a large proportion of your responsibility. Often editors will want each regular municipal and school board meeting in your area covered.

Perhaps other regular meetings of public interest may also be held within your area and thus become your responsibility. For instance, you may be asked to cover meetings of boards of directors at local colleges, vocational schools, or hospitals. And if any large publicly held companies are headquartered in your turf, you may be assigned to cover their annual meetings. In addition, there are the special meetings, such as hearings on the environmental impact of various planned changes and on the use of federal funds for local projects.

Especially if you hold down another full-time job during the day, you may find that meeting coverage is a large portion of your newspaper work. Because most of these meetings are held at night, it will fit into your schedule more easily than other types of coverage.

Some papers, especially morning papers, will ask that you call in the story the night of the meeting. Because of the deadline of some morning papers, you may have to dictate your story before the meeting is over.

Other papers will have no one around late at night to take your dictation and will ask you to phone your story in early the next morning. Still others may ask you to call up that same night and dictate your story to a recording device. That recorded dictation will then be transcribed the next morning when the newspaper's staff return to the job. If you are asked to dictate a story in this way, be sure to speak clearly and to spell each name carefully because there is no one present to ask you to repeat anything that is confusing.

Before attempting to report on a meeting, check carefully how other meetings are being written up in your paper or talk to your editor about how you should cover the session. Some papers view themselves as sort of a paper of record, reporting almost all actions taken by a local governing board. Other editors avoid this approach, arguing it is tedious coverage that is of little interest to the reader. Instead, they would prefer that you single out one or more main points and report on them fully, ignoring the less significant items. The difference in coverage is a reflection of a difference in philosophy as to how papers view their role. It is important that you understand your paper's philosophy in order to know how to proceed.

Singling Out Main Issues

A major challenge in covering meetings is sifting through the large number of issues taken up. It is not unusual for a county board, for instance, to discuss 20 different matters at its regular meeting. The trick is being able to single out the most newsworthy issues and to organize your story effectively.

Remember your reader and consider which issues affect a large number of readers in a significant way. A municipal budget, for instance, is that kind of a newsworthy issue because it determines the local taxes and affects readers' wallets. Environmental issues, such as the location of a county landfill site, are other areas with high news value because of their wide-ranging effect.

Your lead should usually single out the most important issue and report on what the body holding the meeting has done about it. Again, as in the speech story, avoid writing a topic lead that just reports what issue was discussed. Go a step further and tell the reader what happened on that issue.

Usually, your next step will be to develop that lead in your second paragraph. But you may find a couple of major issues were handled during the meeting and you want to let the reader know about the other one before developing information on the primary one. A possible way to handle such a situation is to follow the main lead on the primary issue with a secondary lead on the other important matter. After writing the primary and secondary leads, develop the primary lead, next develop the secondary lead and then proceed to report on what else happened at the meeting.

Some editors will ask you to handle that second main issue in a separate sidebar story with its own headline calling out for the reader's attention. A sidebar is a shorter, related story that is often run alongside the main story. Although related to the larger news story, they are usually of secondary importance. If you do run information on a secondary issue in a sidebar, report only on that issue in the sidebar. Attach any other business that took place at the meeting onto the main story, not to the sidebar. When meetings involve a number of very significant issues, you may need to write more than one sidebar.

Usually, however, you will probably just be writing one story. In covering a meeting, remember that you are not giving a chronological account of what took place. Instead report on the various issues in descending order of importance.

Also remember that you are not a secretary taking minutes. Pick out only information that is newsworthy. The fact that the mayor presided at the council meeting and the meeting started at 7:30 p.m. is not newsworthy.

Do not base your decision on what to emphasize by how much time is devoted to it at the meeting. Sometimes a governmental body can spend an amazing amount of time on the most trivial issue, like deciding on the location of its Christmas party. Just because a lot of time has been devoted to resolving the question does not mean that you should report on that issue. Be especially careful not to get bogged down in reporting discussions of procedure. Emphasize what happened, not the procedure involved.

On the other hand, sometimes the most important matters are acted on quickly with little discussion, in some cases because so much consideration has been given to them at previous meetings. Watch out. Do not let important issues slip by you just because they were dealt with quickly. Sometimes a board may breeze through matters that they would like little attention focused on.

Think of the beginning of each paragraph introducing a new issue as a mini lead. Get directly at what was done about that matter. Report fully on those issues that are of major significance.

If an editor wants you also to report on matters of little news value, you might tag them onto the end of the story with an introductory passage such as "in other action the board," followed by the list of actions.

For instance, you might report:

In other action the board:

—Voted to hire Maxwell Hirschell Inc. of Greenville to repair the roof of the town hall.

   —Decided to postpone action on rezoning of the southern section of Mayville Drive until more information is received from the developer.

   —Awarded a contract for gravel to Malyboo Stone of Marshfield at its low bid of $5,552.

Supplementary Information

If you are unable to accumulate sufficient information on an issue during the meeting, you must gather background on it from other sources.

A key aid often is information prepared in advance of the meeting. Be sure to get your name on a mailing list to receive the agenda before the meeting. As a representative of the media, you will probably have no problem with this request. Often along with a list of the items to be taken up, you will get the specific resolutions to be considered and background information on those issues. Many times the background has been compiled by subcommittees that have considered the issues and are making their recommendations to the full board. Because the full resolutions may not be read at the meeting, it is crucial that you get hold of these resolutions.

Frequently you will need to accumulate more information after the meeting or during a break in the session. It is a good idea to write notes in your margins as a reminder of the things you must check on.

Do not decide you are tired and wait until the next day to collect the background you need. Your task is likely to become much more time consuming if you delay. Most of the people you will need to ask for help with the information are probably at the meeting on the subject. By getting to them there rather than trying to track them all down later, you can save yourself a lot of time.

As you go about your job of making sure all the holes in your story are filled, do not forget about people's names. If you quote what individuals have said at a meeting, your editor will probably want you to identify them. And that means making sure that you have the spelling of their names down correctly. When people identify themselves at a meeting before speaking, do not assume you know how to spell the name without double checking. It might, for instance, be Jon Smythe, not John Smith.

At first the meetings may seem to be hopelessly confusing and you will have many questions you will need to ask to understand what transpired. That is to be expected, especially in the coverage of regular meetings. Those involved have often been working on the issues over the course of many years and are so familiar with them that the background is not rehashed each time they are brought up. But soon you too will become one of the regulars in attendance and will be able to draw upon the background you have gathered during previous meetings of that organization.

You will also find that a lot of what you learn in covering meetings of one governmental body can be carried over to coverage of another such body. You become familiar with terms like "federal block grants" and "industrial revenue bonds" that come up at meetings of many local government bodies.

Because that is true, you will find it helpful to read what reporters covering other meetings are writing. The information in their stories can serve as useful background for yours.

Public Hearings

Coverage of public hearings where many townspeople voice their thoughts on an issue can be especially tough. Try to give your readers an idea of the overall sentiment. Sometimes those present will be asked for a show of hands to indicate how they feel on a subject. Record the results of that hand count. Also try to keep track of how many have testified on each side of an issue.

Identifying speakers at hearings can present a challenge. At some formal hearings people intending to speak will be asked to fill out cards with information including their names. If that is the case, after the meeting you can use those cards to get the spelling of the names of those who spoke. When relevant, report on their affiliation so readers will understand their motivation in speaking out on behalf of one side or another.

As with all meetings, keep your eye on the ball. Look for what is most significant and tell your readers clearly about it.

Generating Other Stories

Because the local experts on a subject often assemble at meetings on an issue, it is a fine place to make contact with helpful sources for future stories. Introduce yourself and ask questions of those individuals even beyond the information you will need for this story. Their responses can make good material for other stories.

Meetings can be a productive spawning ground for future feature stories. If you ever start getting bored with coverage of a meeting, try playing a game with yourself. See if you can come up with at least three good ideas for feature stories triggered by something said at the meeting. You will be surprised how many great possibilities there are if you listen with a creative ear.

Phone Coverage

The time may come when two or more meetings your editor would like you to cover are being held at the same time. You may be asked to pick up the information after the meeting by calling a well-informed source who was present, such as the city clerk. It is difficult to get the same kind of extensive information you can gather by attending the meeting, but it is better than having no story at all.

A few correspondents are handling the dilemma of simultaneous meetings in an interesting way. Working as husband-and-wife teams, one spouse goes to one meeting and the other to the second.

Sometimes an editor may ask you to cover a meeting by phone even if you would have been able to go to it. He or she has decided that it is not worth your time to sit through a whole meeting, especially if the paper is only interested in one issue on the agenda.

As was the case with speech stories, your editor may assign you to write an advance story on a meeting. If so, focus on the most newsworthy topic expected to be discussed and be sure to report the exact time of the meeting.

Rules For Open Meetings

Because you may occasionally be asked by a board to leave a meeting while members consider what they say is confidential information, it is important that you be familiar with your state's regulations requiring open meetings. You may live in a state with stringent rules on when and how public meetings can be closed. Know your rights and use them effectively. Even if your rights are not protected by law, you may be able to make a successful argument that the public should not be excluded from coverage of matters of public interest. But do not make any threats of legal action without first talking to your editor.

C H A P T E R ■ 1 0

POLICE, COURT, AND FIRE NEWS

One of the first things you will need to discuss with your editor is how you should go about covering news of accidents, fires, and crimes. Typically they will be among the most frequent and newsworthy stories you will write.

Editors of some papers, especially those whose stringers are responsible for a large geographic area, may just want you to listen to the radio stations in your area with an ear out for such news. When you hear something your paper may want to use, check in with your editor. If he or she is interested in running the news item, call the appropriate authorities to compile the information and put together a story. Never rely on information reported by other media, although you can use them to alert you to the news occurrence. Always get your facts directly from the authorities.

Editors of many papers will ask their stringers to make regular checks with the authorities to see if anything is going on. Your editor may suggest the various places that should be called and may ask you to check with some of them more than once a day. Occasionally, editors make arrangements with stringers to do this in return for a small fixed salary. Those stringers receive something for their efforts even if no news stories result from their calls. In addition, some stringers monitor police broadcasts, learning about what is going on at the same time as police.

Within any given area, there may be a number of police agencies with which you will have to check. You may, for instance, need to contact the state police, county authorities, and the local municipal police.

Usually you should be able to get information from these authorities over the phone, but the success of this effort will depend on how good your relations are with the local police spokesperson. Most are well aware of their responsibility to inform the citizens of what is going on, and you, a representative of the media, are the path through which they fulfill that responsibility. But occasionally you may encounter some who view such dealings with the media as a waste of their time and an interference with the performance of their job.

Sometimes you may need to go to the police station and use the reports filed by the officers involved. State law varies as to exactly which records you are entitled to see. And the cooperativeness of local authorities in showing reports varies.

In some cases you will need to use other sources in addition to the police. For instance, if accident victims are hospitalized, call the hospital to check on their condition. If someone was killed, check with the coroner to determine the cause of death.

Find out from your editor what types of information you should report. For instance, how serious must an accident be to warrant a story in your paper? Some newspapers may only use accidents in which someone is killed. Others may only report an accident if someone has been injured or killed or if the dollar value of the damage is above a certain amount. A theft may be reported only if the value of the object or objects stolen is over a certain amount. To a large extent, the cutoff point will be determined by the size of the circulation of the paper. The larger papers will be more selective in the type of stories they use because they do not have enough space to report all the less serious incidents that take place within their circulation area.

After deciding to report on an incident, you will have to determine which information from the report to include. Generally in smaller towns anyone killed or seriously injured is identified as is anyone charged with a crime. Be careful not to report the name of someone being questioned about a crime before that individual has been formally charged by authorities, except in unusual circumstances—and in those cases, check with your editor on how to proceed.

When identifying someone involved in an accident or charged with a crime, most papers will do so by using the name, age, and address.

The exact time when the incident took place should also be reported, although not in the lead because the precise numbers will tend to distract the reader and make the lead difficult to read. Just indicate what day the incident took place in your lead.

Accidents

Checklists of the kinds of information that are typically included will remind you of significant details that must be accumulated. Let's look at accident reporting first. Generally include the following:

- Location of accident (often by indicating on what road it took place, the nearest crossroad, and the distance from that crossroad)
- Direction the vehicle or vehicles were headed
- Time
- Other circumstances
- Identification of driver or drivers
- Identification of anyone killed or injured, cause of death, extent of injuries and the hospital where the injured are being treated, if they are hospitalized
- Type of vehicles (not the make of the vehicle, unless it has relevant news value, but whether it was a car, truck, motorcycle)
- Charges placed, if any
- Amount of bail
- Upcoming court proceedings

Look for unusual circumstances about the incident to include in your lead. Especially be on the lookout for patterns that suggest a safety hazard. For instance, if three traffic fatalities have occurred at the same corner during the course of the year, emphasize that, and get comments on it.

Fires

Although police may sometimes be able to help you with information on local fires, you will generally have to contact the firefighters to get a thorough account of the incident.

For correspondents who are covering less densely populated areas, reaching the local firefighters may sometimes prove difficult. In these areas the firefighting responsibilities are typically handled by volunteer fire departments whose members have full-time jobs elsewhere. The volunteer fire chief may be back out plowing his fields, far removed from a telephone, by the time you hear about a fire and try to track him down to get the facts about it.

In metropolitan areas, however, there are full-time firefighters and sometimes one person specifically assigned to respond to media questions. When possible, it is also a good idea to talk to the firefighters in charge of fighting the fire and, if it is a different individual, the firefighter heading up any investigation of the fire's cause.

Because a fire can smolder a long time, keeping firefighters on the scene to make sure it does not flare up again, it may be hours later before they can return to the fire station and file a report. Thus, you may have to go out to the scene of the fire to get information. And frequently it is a good idea anyway to do that kind of on-the-scene reporting in covering fires. They can be very dramatic events involving heroism, human pathos, and occasionally loss of life as well as property.

Do not neglect to round out your story by checking with other sources when necessary. You may have to call the hospital on injured individuals, contact owners of property on what their plans are and whether their loss was covered by insurance, and ask agencies such as the Red Cross what is being done to help the victims.

Possible information for stories includes these facts about the fire:

- Location
- Time
- Identification of anyone killed or injured, cause of death, extent of injuries and the hospital where the injured are being treated, if they are hospitalized
- Information on any humans or pets in the building when the fire started
- Cause of fire, including whether arson is suspected and why
- Circumstances, including where it started, how it spread, how it was discovered
- Fire units that responded to the call, equipment used
- Rescue operations
- Description by witnesses
- Charges placed, if any
- Circumstances of arrest
- Amount of bail
- Upcoming court proceedings
- Description of loss, including estimate of cost of damage
- Information on whether a business that suffered a fire will continue to operate

Be careful in reporting on the cause of fires. The appropriate fire department spokesperson should be used as the source of information for the cause, and the information on the cause must be attributed to that person.

Also watch how you handle estimates of the extent of damage. The amount may become the subject of controversy between the owner and the insurance company, and a precise figure is hard to determine until much later. Be sure to report whose estimate you are using, attributing the figure to that individual.

Crimes

Crimes can be tricky to report, especially if someone has been charged. You must make sure you do not inadvertently say that a suspect is guilty of a crime. Those accused are presumed innocent until proved guilty.

Do not say that "John Smith has been arrested for murder" because it suggests that he actually committed that murder, even though he has not been found guilty. You might instead say "John Smith has been accused of murder," "John Smith has been charged with murder," or "John Smith has been arrested in connection with the murder of. . . ." Similarly, do not refer to him as the "accused murderer" because that too suggests that he actually is the murderer.

Most editors will tell you not to identify the victims of sexual assault—by name or in any other way that will single them out. The reason is that, sadly, a stigma is attached to the victim and the rule against identification is to protect that victim. In some cases, this guideline may mean that you cannot very thoroughly describe the crime. If a father is accused of incest, for instance, stating that charge can identify the victim of the crime.

Most papers do not use confessions until they are admitted in open court. When you think of how many people have confessed to famous murders, like the Son of Sam killings, you will understand why papers have set up this guideline. There are many troubled individuals who seem to welcome celebrity status even if it means confessing to a heinous crime they did not commit. Papers do, however, sometimes report that someone who confessed made a statement to police, without revealing the nature of that statement.

Because they may result in unfair pretrial publicity, many papers also will not use opinions about a defendant's character or guilt or innocence or information about a prior criminal record.

Homicides, Assaults

Here's a checklist to use in compiling information on a homicide or assault. Use it as a starting point for information that might be relevant to a story you are working on.

- Identification of victim
- Extent of injuries, cause of death
- Location of incident
- Time of incident
- Circumstances, including any weapon that might have been used

- Description of suspect, if being sought
- Charges placed, if any
- Circumstances of arrest
- Amount of bail
- Upcoming court proceedings

Thefts

One of the more common types of crimes you will be asked to report on involves theft. Here is a checklist that might prove helpful in the reporting of such crimes, including burglaries (when a building is illegally entered) and robberies (when someone's goods or money are stolen with the use or threat of force).

- Type of items taken
- Value of items taken
- Location of incident
- Time of incident
- Identification of victim
- Past thefts incurred by victim
- Circumstances, including weapon used
- Injuries and how they were caused
- Description of suspect, if being sought
- Charges placed, if any
- Circumstances of arrest
- Amount of bail
- Upcoming court proceedings

Usually the items stolen and their value will be a major focus in the lead. If someone has been charged with the crime, report that in your lead.

Courts

You may have to do a follow-up story on the crime when the accused ends up in court. Some of you will have to cover courts and others will not. Much of the more newsworthy local court action takes place on a county level, and some papers staff the court scene there with full-time reporters. Those of you who are covering all the news of your counties and perhaps other nearby counties without assistance from the regular staff will probably be assigned to report on the court system in those counties.

Ask your editor how you are to cover the courts, if they are your responsibility. Should you regularly check the court docket or just keep track of the schedule of important cases you know to be upcoming. This too will vary from one paper to another.

Covering the legal system is a complicated task. A book entitled *The Reporter and the Law* by Lyle W. Denniston (1980) is of great assistance in reporting on the courts. Another very helpful tool is *Law and the Courts* designed with journalists in mind by the American Bar Association.[1]

There are two bodies of law, civil (in which an individual usually initiates an action) and criminal (in which the government is the accuser). You may occasionally get involved in covering civil proceedings. You might, for instance, be assigned to cover a dispute over a will involving a wealthy and prominent local family, an employment discrimination case, or a contract dispute. But it is usually criminal suits that have the greatest news interest and are therefore the ones you will be covering most often.

Many of the cases you will be working on will never go to trial because a large proportion are plea bargained. That is, prosecutors make arrangements with defendants to reduce the charges in return for a guilty plea. The arrangement helps to alleviate crowded court dockets and to ensure that the defendant will not get off scot-free. In part because of this system, many court reporters spend a considerable amount of their time talking to court officials and lawyers rather than attending a trial.

And even when a case does go to trial, it is rare that a newspaper editor will consider it worthwhile for you to sit through the proceedings from beginning to end. Only the most newsworthy, dramatic cases are likely to get that kind of treatment.

If you are going to spend some time covering a trial, be aware that the opening and closing arguments of the attorneys involved can present some of the most helpful information. In their opening statements they lay out for the jury what they hope to establish during the proceedings, often indicating the kind of evidence they plan to introduce. Those statements can be the basis of a good story at the outset of the trial.

And the concluding arguments are frequently very dramatically delivered and emotion-laden summations and entreaties for action on the part of the jury. Try to be present when both the prosecuting and defense attorneys deliver their

---

[1]*Law and the Courts* is available by writing the American Bar Association, Order Department, 750 N. Lake Shore Drive, Chicago, IL 60611. The cost is $2. It includes a glossary of legal terms and a description of procedures involved in civil and criminal cases.

summations. You must take great care in ensuring that your coverage is even-handed, and it would be difficult to achieve such fairness if you were present to hear only one side of the case.

Throughout the course of writing your stories, remember that the defendant must be presumed innocent until proved guilty. Do not just single out the damaging evidence and ignore the defense's response. Be careful to attribute all testimony.

Testimony often is conflicting, and one version is a lie. In covering court proceedings, you have protection from libel in reporting these falsehoods. Reporters using information that is entered into court records are protected by what is called *qualified privilege*. Because of the need to ensure a free exchange of ideas, statements at government meetings are similarly protected by qualified privilege.

Trials may go on for days. You will frequently find yourself writing a story on deadline as the proceedings are continuing. You are often writing the latest segment of a running story that may have been reported on before during earlier days of court proceedings and also at the point when the crime occurred and someone was arrested in connection with it. But assume readers have not read any of the earlier stories and provide sufficient background information that they can understand what is going on. Because you want to stress the latest development each day, often the best bet for your lead is to emphasize an especially newsworthy bit of information that was entered into the proceedings during the past day. In some cases the best lead may be a summary of the proceedings that took place since your last deadline.

Exact quotes of those testifying and descriptions of what they are wearing and how the jury reacted to them can add a lot to your coverage.

The legal world can be a very complicated place. One of your greatest challenges in covering courts will be to explain these complicated proceedings in a way that the reader can easily understand. Define legal terms and explain the significance of various actions. Be on the lookout for a pattern of tactics used by attorneys during trials and explain them to your readers. Often you will need to try to interview the attorneys to help you with this and other information.

To be able to explain the proceedings clearly to your readers and describe their significance, you will have to understand them thoroughly yourself.

As a starting point, you will need to understand the makeup of the court system you are covering. There is a federal court system, which includes federal district courts, the circuit courts of appeals, and the Supreme Court. But it is unlikely any of those courts will be in the geographic area you are covering.

Probably your main concern will be coverage of local courts as well as special courts such as small claims and children's court. The names of these various courts will vary from one state to another. Be sure to report fully and accurately the name of the court in which the proceedings are taking place.

Pretrial

The first time you may see a defendant appear in court may be at a *preliminary hearing*. (In other areas different terms, including arraignment, are used for this initial appearance.) In this proceeding the suspect is usually advised of his or her rights.

Procedures as well as terms for these initial encounters vary from one area to another. In some jurisdictions a judge may also determine at that hearing whether there are reasonable grounds or probable cause to believe that a crime has been committed and that the accused committed the offense. In many jurisdictions a proceeding commonly called an *arraignment* is held after the initial appearance. At that arraignment the accused is generally asked to plead to the charge.

After the defendant is formally accused, there are several kinds of motions that may be filed by attorneys before a trial gets underway. For instance, the defense attorney may file a motion for change of venue, arguing the defendant cannot receive a fair trial in that judicial area and asking that the proceedings be moved to another location.

Trial Procedure

Before a jury trial can get underway, a jury must be selected. Sometimes this selection process may yield interesting stories. Attorneys are well aware of the importance of having sympathetic jurors and sometimes try to ask revealing questions to determine whom to select. They are allowed to challenge the seating of jurors, but within prescribed guidelines. They can strike a juror for cause when they establish specific grounds for disqualification. But they are also given a number of challenges allowing them to eliminate a person for no reason. Those are called *peremptory challenges*, and the number allowed each attorney is usually set by statute.

Because the trial procedure follows an established pattern, you can know what to expect will happen in what order and thus have some idea of when to check back for an update. First the prosecuting and defense attorneys make opening statements. Then the prosecution presents its case. If at the end of that presentation, the judge determines the public prosecutor has not established a case by presenting sufficient proof, he or she directs a verdict of acquittal.

If the trial continues, the defense may then call witnesses to rebut the prosecution's charges. And after both sides have had a chance to present their cases and question and cross-examine witnesses, the attorneys make their closing arguments.

The judge instructs the jury, and the jury heads to the privacy of the jury room to deliberate. Of course the outcome of its deliberations will likely be the most newsworthy aspect of the trial. Depending on how the story breaks, you may have to keep checking back regularly to see if it has reached a verdict. If the verdict is reached before your deadline, your editor will be unhappy if you miss it.

Except in the rare cases in which a judge gags a jury and instructs them not to talk to reporters, you are free to interview them and try to find out what sort of concerns were raised in the jury room and why they decided as they did. And although judges will often decline to be interviewed during the proceedings, many will answer questions after the proceedings are completed.

The judge may decide on a sentence right after the verdict or may wait several days as information on the background of the accused is compiled to help in deciding on the appropriate sentence.

After all of that, the case may be appealed. But often that follow-up story is out of your hands because the appellate court is likely to be located outside your area.

Nonetheless, that may not be the end of the story as far as you are concerned. You may find yourself involved in other follow-up stories. For instance, you may interview the accused later in prison and get the individual's reaction to what transpired. Or you may do a follow-up story on the relatives and friends of the victim and their reaction to the way justice was administered. And someday you might be doing a feature story on what society hopes is the rehabilitated criminal returning to society for a fresh start.

There is a lot of human emotion and drama in the nation's courtrooms. If you tried to make up a fictional story, it would be hard to come up with anything as seemingly far-fetched as many a trial. It beats the colorfulness of a lot of soap operas. Be sure that human side comes through in your accounts. Do not get bogged down in high-faluting foreign phrases like *nolo contendere, voir dire,* and *prima facie* that are so prevalent in the court scene. Remember your reader.

USING PRESS RELEASES,
REPORTS, SURVEYS

Although much of the information in your stories will have been gathered from interviews, sometimes written material may serve as the main basis. Press releases from service organizations, churches, school organizations, companies; reports by governmental agencies, consultants, community organizations; surveys by professional pollsters, local officials—all have potential news value.

For a new reporter accustomed to academic research done largely through books and periodicals, using interviews as a major part of the research calls for a big change in approach to researching. But in the course of switching to that reliance on interviews, some reporters forget about the value of information in written form. Someone with knowledge on the subject has taken considerable time to collect and write up the information. Admittedly, it is often written with a different purpose in mind than that of the reporter, who is after an objective, newsworthy story. But it offers a good starting point for a reporter rounding up information for an article.

Press Releases

Let's first take a look at use of press releases. Aware of the need for a good public image, a wide variety of institutions, companies, and individuals are hiring public relations staffs to help polish that image. The U.S. government is among the largest employers of those public relations specialists, disparagingly referred to as flacks by some beleaguered journalists who are the target of their efforts.

According to Tom G. Palmer, director of student affairs at the Institute for Humane Studies, the Pentagon alone had 1,066 full-time PR people. Writing in *The Wall Street Journal* in 1985, he also reported that the Agriculture Department employed 144 full-time public-affairs staffers and if you included the subagencies, the number mounted to 704. The Education Department had a staff of 46, and the Department of Transportation had 21.

Former Senator William Proxmire, with his Golden Fleece Award, has been among the masters of the successful press release. Regularly he has given out his award to a government entity for what he says is its contribution to wasting taxpayer money.

A former journalist, he knew just the kind of information that would captivate the media. Waste of government money would generally get nice-sized headlines. Making it a regular award secured him high visibility as the presenter of the award. And dubbing it the Golden Fleece Award gave it the kind of colorfulness the media go for.

His unsuccessful opponent for the Senate seat, Scott McCallum, also realizing the news value of the award, selected Proxmire for the Silver Turkey Award.

It is fine for the news media to draw upon press releases like the Golden Fleece Award for their daily fare. Their staffers cannot be everywhere, and they are heavily dependent on information provided by such releases. That information can be a valuable addition to their pages.

But they must be careful not to be manipulated by the issuers of the press releases. Often the releases should just be a starting point, a tipoff to a good, usable story. Much additional information frequently must be gathered. For instance, a reporter must make sure that a government agency receiving a Golden Fleece Award has had a chance to explain its spending. It may have a good justification for how the funds are used.

And the story appearing in the paper must be in a well-written news format. Although many public relations representatives for news figures like Proxmire may want to get their bosses' names in the lead, a good reporter will rewrite the release to emphasize the main action taken or idea espoused instead of that name. The complimentary subjective adjectives, like "beautiful," "exciting," and "fascinating," which so frequently turn up in press releases, are weeded out. And other non-newsworthy information also has to go.

As you become known as a stringer around your community, your mailbox may start to fill up with press releases. That is good. Encourage publicity people to keep them coming. But be careful to add any additional information needed and rewrite them before passing them along to your editor.

The use of such publicity releases may cause you some of your greatest problems in dealing with the public. Individuals in charge of publicity for an organization feel a responsibility to their colleagues in that organization to make sure they get publicity into the newspaper. If they give you something and they do not see it in the paper, you are likely to hear from them because they will be hearing about it from other group members.

Take time to explain to these individuals how your newspaper works. For instance, it may have a policy not to use notices of meetings at which nothing beyond regular business is planned. Or perhaps it runs a calendar of such meetings, but the copy has to be submitted by a certain date for the meeting to make it into the paper. Describe those policies to the publicity representatives.

You will also have to explain that ultimately it is up to your editor, not you, to determine what gets into the paper. And that editor's selection may be based on how much other news is competing for space. As a result, a release on a certain subject might be run one day but not on another when the news load is heavy. The decision is likely to look arbitrary to organization members who may accuse you of being unfair to them. If you can clearly explain the process to them, you will help prevent their annoyance with the paper and their complaints to you.

Some newspapers are holding annual workshops for publicity people. Here the editors explain the paper's policy and give suggestions for the kinds of information that is considered newsworthy. If your paper conducts such workshops, familiarize people in your area with them and encourage them to attend.

Editors have changed their attitudes over the years as to the kind of information on community organizations they will include. In some papers, the trend had been away from devoting so much space to community events. That meant stringers, especially in many smaller communities, might have seen a dramatic decrease in the amount of stories they were able to get into the paper.

But in recent years editors have been starting to rethink their paper's role. Even editors of some of the larger metro papers have decided that perhaps they should devote more space to serving as a community bulletin board. In part, their decision has no doubt been affected by competition from television. They are trying to emphasize the kinds of service they can provide and television cannot. Some editors have decided this is one of those areas.

Reports

Although zealous public relations people are laboring to call your attention to the press releases they would like to get published, another form of written information, the study or report, may elude your notice. Often a tremendous amount of work has been put into the preparation of a study by a leading expert or group of experts on the subject. But the specialists who did the work might consider it unprofessional to ballyhoo their efforts to the press or may not realize that what they have done has any news value. Or those involved may, because of the results of the findings, prefer that the information not receive any press attention.

Even if the report is something its writer would prefer you not see, many reports are public documents and therefore available to you on request. For instance, your city government officials may have been contemplating the possibility of building a convention center in the downtown area. Outside consultants are hired to examine the feasibility of such a project. They examine what possible conventions might be held in the city, how many rooms are available for participants at local hotels and motels, what the effect of a convention center would be on the downtown area, how much such a project would cost and how it would be financed. The report was paid for by the taxpayers. Its findings belong to the taxpayers and thus you are entitled to see it and report on it.

Frequent sources of important news are reports on the environmental impact of various facilities planned for your local area. If, for instance, there is a possibility that a prison may land in your town, statutes may require that studies be done of the possible impact of the facility on the environment around it. Those studies are likely to include examination of a wider range of areas than you might have imagined. Such a study might, for instance, project how many construction and new full-time jobs would be added because of the new facility. Also considered might be the extent of increased revenue expected to be brought into the community by the new employees' salaries and purchases of supplies for the institution, the projected increase in residential units needed, and the anticipated effect of the increased traffic on roads in the area.

Regional planning commissions often prepare reports of newsworthy interest. For instance, they might examine the impact of a proposed abandonment of a railroad line crisscrossing the area, the need for extensions of thruways, and the trends in the growth or decline in population of local cities and in types of retailing establishments in those areas.

Local police departments come up with interesting annual figures on crimes in the area. You can use them to compare the number of violent crimes during the most recent year with previous years. And you can take a look at their total arrest record and compare it with years gone by.

Companies are often very secretive about their financial dealings. But if they are publicly traded, the Securities and Exchange Commission (SEC) requires that they make certain types of information available to the public. Much newsworthy information may turn up in their annual reports, which have to be prepared in compliance with SEC guidelines. In those reports you learn their profits or losses and total sales for the year. If they have been sued, the annual report will tell you about the litigation. And the report of the financial condition of the company prepared by an outside auditor also has to be included. Often, too, the companies use the annual report to tout new products about to be sold and make predictions for the upcoming year. These can generate some good possible news tips.

Learn how to use reports effectively. They may have tables of contents, but those sometimes are not very helpful. Do not rely on them too heavily. Skim through the whole report, and you may be surprised what you find. Remember that the writer of the report has a much different function than you, the journalist. As a result, some of the most fascinating tidbits of information may be buried amid other very mundane material. You may even uncover several such nuggets, each of which can be developed into good, worthwhile separate stories.

Sometimes the passages of greatest significance can be hidden amid more scientific and technical information that will have little meaning to the general public. Take this passage about PCBs (polychlorinated biphenyls, which are toxic substances suspected of causing a variety of health problems) prepared by a Toxic Substance Task Force:

> Studies of species shifts in composition related to PCBs have not been evaluated. The water flea, "Daphnia magna," suffered 50 percent reproductive impairment when exposed under continuous-flow conditions to Aroclor 1248 at 2.1 ug-L and to Aroclor 1254 at 1.3 ug-L. From the same study using Aroclor 1254, survival of the midge, "Tanytasus dissimilis," was reduced by 50 percent at o.45 ug-L. Invertebrate life in the Fox River and lower Green Bay have been devastated by past pollution. The cause of this devastation has been mainly attributed to organic pollution and low dissolved oxygen. However, acute or chronic toxicity from PCB contamination is also likely.

The reporter who managed to wade through all of the technical information to the last two sentences will encounter an important opinion that he or she might otherwise have missed. That is, toxic waste may be contributing to the devastation of invertebrate life in local waterways. That life is perhaps being harmed not only by the more ordinary organic pollution that had been blamed but also quite possibly by PCB toxic waste.

Your job of writing up the report will often call for interviewing of appropriate experts, perhaps those who prepared the study, to provide supplemental information. Sometimes you will need to talk to others not involved with the report's preparation to get their reactions to what is contained within it.

The lead should focus on the most newsworthy findings in the report. And toward the beginning of the story, probably about the second paragraph, carefully explain the background of the report. Who compiled it, who funded it, what purpose is it to serve, who will act on its recommendations or findings? Much of the report may contain judgments. Be careful to attribute them appropriately.

Reports may consist of largely statistical material. Many individuals with a great facility with words at the same time seem to have a fear of numbers. You may be one of them. Do not be frightened by the numbers. Study them, looking for patterns and trends. Try to fathom their significance. Explain the numbers to the readers in a way that they can readily understand. For instance, if you are examining how taxes in your municipality have risen over the years, report how the amount has increased for the owner of an average-priced home.

Reporting the percent of increase or decrease in taxes, prices, profits, crimes, accidents, and other information can be a good addition to a story. Remember that in making the computations, compare the amount of change with the original figure, not the most recent number. Subtract and find out the difference between the figures for each of the 2 years, then divide that difference by the original amount. For instance, if there were 100 burglaries reported in 1989 and 125 in 1990, the number of those crimes rose 25%. You can compute that amount by subtracting 100 from 125, then dividing the difference (25) by the original amount (100).

At the same time you report the percent of change, be sure you tell the reader what the latest figure is. If you report, for instance, that housing starts are up 50% over last year, the reader will also need to know how many houses have been built. Is the number up from 2 to 3, perhaps, or from 40 to 60?

When wading through figures, be especially on the lookout for record amounts. Remember that in making news judgments, you are looking for the unusual. If something has set a record, it is indeed unusual.

Be careful not to hit the reader with a barrage of numbers. Instead, intersperse them amid other information. If it is crucial that you bunch up a lot of numbers, consider doing it in list form, similar to the sports pages' box scores.

Double check carefully all numbers you use in a story. It is very easy to make a typographical error that will distort the story significantly. Add an extra zero by mistake and you end up with a 100% instead of a 10% increase, for instance.

If you are drawing information from charts, be especially careful to look at the guide accompanying them. Often numbers in parentheses contained in financial statements indicate red ink. That is, those numbers are losses, and you will be telling a very different story if you erred and reported them as profits. Sometimes, too, you may notice in small letters above a chart that the numbers listed are in millions or thousands. Be careful to look for such explanations.

USA Today has been leading the way in using graphs and tables to illustrate its stories. If you are working for a paper that is following that lead, be on the lookout for those kinds of illustrations to submit with your stories. They can be extremely helpful in assisting readers to understand the numbers and appreciate their significance.

Surveys

The reporting of surveys has also become a frequent feature of newspaper pages, with the help of computers to compile the results.

Some newspapers are compiling their own survey results. Larger metro papers even hire experts in survey techniques. Because hundreds of individuals generally have to be questioned to ensure the accuracy of surveys, a lot of staff time can go into conducting them. Occasionally you may be asked to help out.

More frequently you may find yourself in the position of writing a story based on survey information compiled by someone else. Maybe the local political candidate has had a survey conducted to sample the kind of support he has and the likelihood he will win the elected office he is seeking. Or perhaps the local Chamber of Commerce has studied area flying needs in an effort to lure a new air carrier to your community.

The results of such surveys can have great news value. But you have to be careful how you report them.

Be sure you report who has sponsored the survey. The reader needs to know, for instance, if it was conducted by the candidate's campaign staff or the League of Women Voters. The campaign staff has an interest in seeing the candidate win the election whereas the League of Women Voters is nonpartisan. As a result, a survey by that organization might have greater credibility.

Also report how many were questioned. Never misrepresent the extent of a survey. The so-called man-on-the street survey, in which perhaps a half-dozen individuals are asked for their opinions, can be a good newspaper story. But you must make sure you are in no way suggesting that it is a scientifically conducted survey that indicates anything beyond what the few people interviewed think.

Sometimes you may also need to report the circumstances under which the survey was conducted. How were people selected as respondents to the survey? Were people asked to respond by mail, over the phone, in person? What was the exact question or questions asked?

When was the survey conducted? As we have seen from past political campaigns, the timing can make a tremendous difference in the results. Voters have been known to change their minds dramatically during the last weekend before an election, especially if a major event involving the candidate takes place during that time. The results of a survey can quickly become outdated.

Report on the margin for error, if you have that information. Many of the surveying firms hired to conduct the surveys can give you that figure.

Surveys vary in the extent of the range of responses possible. Some surveys will limit the respondents' choices to two. They will, for instance, be asked which of two candidates they support, whether they agree or disagree with a statement. Sometimes they will be given a bit wider choice of responses. They may be asked if they strongly agree, agree, disagree, or strongly disagree with a statement. Such types of limited-choice questionnaires enable the results to be tabulated easily.

But sometimes surveyors will try to get at feelings they do not think can be recorded by this limited kind of response. Instead, they will ask respondents open-ended questions that will enable them to answer with anything that comes to mind. For instance, they might be asked to evaluate how effectively they think the president is doing his job.

Other questionnaires may combine the limited and open-ended type of responses. Individuals might be asked which of two political candidates they favor and why.

In writing up the results of the survey, your lead will report on the findings. Use numbers tallying up the results of limited-choice questions. If open-ended questions were used, develop your story using some of the responses to these questions. Report the sentiments of the majority first, then follow with the minority's thoughts.

Political surveys have been at the center of controversy in journalism circles in recent years. Some charge they unduly influence the results of races and argue surveys measuring support for candidates should not be used before the election. Concern is expressed that surveys may have the effect of creating a landslide as voters who have not made up their mind decide to go with the front-runner singled out by the surveys. Others worry that the front-runner may lose votes, arguing that voters will think they do not have to bother to head to the polls because their candidate is a shoo-in and does not need their vote. It may take extensive surveying on the effect of surveys to resolve the controversy.

NEWS CONFERENCES

We still often call them *press conferences*. But in many instances the television media, with their piercing lights and cumbersome cameras filling the front of the room, tend to dominate the event. Because they have to so great an extent become television phenomena, *news conference* is today a more appropriate term.

But no matter what you call them, they can be very important sources of news, and you often need to be there. Make sure that those who might schedule news conferences know how to reach you. Among them are the district attorney; the police chief; the mayor; the director of the Chamber of Commerce; and leaders of protest organizations, such as pro-choice and anti-abortion, environmental, and feminist groups.

Why Hold News Conferences?

In some cases the reason for disseminating information by this method is to save time. A police chief besieged with the same questions about a murder from all of the local media, for instance, may decide to answer all the questions at one designated time. Anyone calling for information is asked to show up at the news conference to get it.

In other cases the motivation may be a bid for publicity. By staging a news conference, publicity people can create a news event. They are all too aware of the competitive and herd instinct of the media. If one paper or station covers a news conference, it becomes news and the other media representatives feel they have missed something if they, too, are not providing coverage. It is rare that media will turn down an invitation to a news conference, even if they do not know what subject will be discussed. Try to find out in advance what will be taken up to help your editor decide if the subject justifies the time it will take to cover it.

Preparation

If you are assigned to cover the event, read up on the subject, if you can in the time allowed, and prepare a list of questions to ask. In drawing up your questions, remember you will need the more routine information, such as ages and addresses of those accused of crimes, as well as more colorful facts.

Often the conference will begin with a statement from the individual holding it and is then opened up for questions. Frequently the statement will set the agenda for much of the questioning. But be careful not to allow that to happen if there are other important lines of questioning that should be directed at the respondent. Be aware of the background of the individual and consider whether there are other areas about which he or she should be asked.

Remember that you must get control over the kind of information being disseminated. At a news conference, assuming that control is more difficult than in a one-on-one interview session. The individuals conducting the news conference have more power in setting the agenda. They can call on reporters known to be more sympathetic or less hard-hitting in their questioning. And the fact that the questioner may not be able to ask a series of questions makes it difficult to explore and probe a subject.

The presidential news conference is a prime example of weaknesses of the event as a way of gathering information. The president selects from scores of reporters allowed in the room the few questioners he would like to ask a question. The event may only last a half hour, and the range of questioners is further limited by the tradition of allowing representatives of the three major television networks and the wire services to be among those selected to question the president.

Covering the president is especially maddening because the news conference is about the only time a reporter is able to talk to the president directly. Much of the time the administration's policies are set forth by his aides.

Special Problems

It is unlikely that you will be in the position of questioning the president. But your problems at a news conference are the same. You must try to do what reporters at presidential press conferences are criticized for not doing—follow up on the questions of others. Listen carefully to what is being said. Do not just go with a showy question in mind that you hope you will have a chance to ask. If someone stirs up some interesting material but does not have a chance to ask more questions to develop it, jump in and ask the necessary questions.

The problems in covering a news conference can be aggravated by the presence of a lot of television reporters. They are aware of the need for the camera to capture them asking a question and getting a response that will work well for showing in their report, and that concern is likely to determine their actions, sometimes to the detriment of other reporters.

Another problem with getting information from a news conference is it is tough to get a competitive edge over your fellow newspeople. When you conduct an interview, your story is only as good as the information elicited through your questioning. If you did not think of the right question to ask, you are not likely to get the information. But at a news conference, all reporters are drawing from the information produced by the joint questioning. The competition shares in the fruits of your labor. As a result, if you think you have a question that would get at significant information that might be overlooked by others, you might want to save that question and ask it after the news conference is over.

Also after the conference you may need to talk to others not present at the session to provide additional information for the story. If the person conducting the conference made charges against someone, get in touch with that target of the criticism for a response. Depending on the situation, the information provided at the news conference may not even turn out to be your best bet for the lead. Perhaps it will be just a starting point for what will turn out to be a better story based on other information.

And sometimes the information from the news conference does not turn out to have any news value. If you think that perhaps it does not warrant a story, tell your editor and seek instructions on how to handle it.

If you do file a story, your lead should, of course, report the most significant information gathered. Much of the challenge in reporting on the event is similar to covering a speech. You will need to weave together good direct and indirect quotes. Be careful to organize your information carefully, getting at the most newsworthy areas first.

Although it has its shortcomings, the news conference can provide access to sources that you might otherwise not have, such as the president.

The custom of having the president respond at a news conference is peculiarly American. And that custom only originated as recently as the beginning of this century. Now it is so entrenched that if a president goes several months without scheduling a conference, he is subject to criticism for not making himself accountable enough to the American public.

Like those reporters who have clamored for greater access to the president, you as a watchdog of your community must make sure local officials are providing adequate public information. Use news conferences effectively to help provide some of that information. But do not rely on them too heavily without supplementing the information you receive there.

OBITUARIES

Local citizens have a good chance of making the pages of your paper at least twice in their lives—when they are born and when they die—and perhaps, if they decide to go that route, when they marry.

The selection of individuals whose obituaries will be used depends to a large extent on the size of the paper. Having one's obituary included in the pages of *The New York Times* is the mark of a successful life. The paper covering the country's largest city does not have enough space to record the deaths of all its citizens. It has to select only the most prominent. But a smaller paper is likely to use obituaries of anyone who had lived within its circulation area. And you as a stringer may be responsible for accumulating that information.

Compiling the Information

Check with your editor about how it should be handled. Some newspapers these days, looking for new ways to make money, are running only obituaries that are purchased and written by the purchaser. But if you are working for a paper that provides obituaries as a news service for its readers, inquire about how the information should be rounded up. Are you expected to call each funeral home within your area each day to see if its staff has any obituaries to report? Or should you perhaps make sure that the directors of those establishments know where to reach you and just wait to be called by them? Because it is part of the service they provide for the bereaved family, they can be expected to be fairly dependable in getting in touch with you and providing the information.

Some may have their own standard forms they use in compiling the information, or perhaps your newspaper has forms they would like you to distribute to the funeral homes.

At the Ogden (Utah) *Standard-Examiner* obituaries are sent directly to the newspaper's computers by funeral homes using their own computers. Because of the time saved and possible errors avoided, we can expect many other papers will soon start using this method.

If you are accumulating information on a death, be careful that it is accurate. Family scrapbooks will be preserving the newspaper clippings of a relative's demise long after you have stopped stringing.

And, sadly, you have to be careful to avoid being taken in by hoaxes. Throughout the country there are those who delight in calling in fake obituaries—be it of their friends or enemies. As a result, papers have established methods for making sure the obituary is legitimate. Some will use only information obtained from a known funeral home. Rules may require that if information is provided by another source, the death must be confirmed by checking with members of the family.

Newspapers that consider themselves papers of record may try to run obituaries of all deaths in the area. But obituaries have a further function in addition to just serving as a public record. You may be surprised to learn that studies have found obituaries are among the most widely read items in the paper.

For those who have made real contributions to the community and the country, the obituary offers a chance to have their deeds set forth for public notice. In preparation for the death of leading citizens, many papers collect biographical information from them and keep it on file. The wire services compile information on key national figures, especially those getting up in years, in case of their sudden demise. If the president were to die today, stories would be immediately available to mark his death and recall his contributions.

Formula for Obituaries

Just as the funeral is a tradition-bound way of marking the death, so too is the typical obituary. Many papers will follow a prescribed formula in reporting the information and run those obituaries in the alphabetical order of the names of the deceased. But deaths of more well-known individuals may be treated differently. The information may be reported in stories that look and read like regular news stories.

Because newspapers generally follow a prescribed style for reporting on deaths, it is important that you examine that formula carefully and follow it when you write up death notices. That style will differ somewhat from paper to paper. But many will follow a style similar to the one described here.

Lead

Begin with a lead that identifies deceased individuals by name and reports on their main accomplishments during their lives. In many cases that accomplishment will be their job. In other cases it may be their efforts on behalf of a charity or a cause. In determining what to use, try to decide on the feat for which they were best known.

Sometimes the background included in the lead represented only a very small part of a person's life, yet gained him or her considerable notoriety. For example, the *Chicago Tribune* obituary writer decided the accomplishment for which William J. Barry was best known was that he was "said to have been the first person to dye the Chicago River green for the city's St. Patrick's Day celebration." That fact about his life was included in the lead of his obituary.

The *Tribune*'s obituary on Frank Oppenheimer identified him in the lead as "physicist and pioneering educator who, like his brother, was the target of federal investigations during the McCarthy era." Alhough the McCarthy era was decades ago, Oppenheimer was still likely to have been best known for his role in those investigations.

The age should also be included in the lead as should the day of death. Many papers will also use the date in parentheses following the day of the week because the articles are often saved for posterity, and the date is not otherwise likely to appear in the portion of the paper that has been cut out.

A typical lead might read: John Smith, 68, of Hiltonville, a dentist here for 40 years, died Monday (Nov. 16, 1986).

Some papers will report the cause of death. Others will report merely that the individual died after a short- or long-term illness.

Other Information

The lead is followed by a paragraph or series of paragraphs describing the biographical background of the individual. Look carefully at the obituaries in the paper for which you are writing to see how detailed a description is included. Typically, obituaries will report various jobs held by the individual, military service, any public office held, education, and involvement in church and other community work.

The next section will report on surviving relatives. The section can be introduced by "surviving are," "he is survived by," or "survivors are" followed by a colon. The listing of relatives follows a designated order determined by their closeness to the deceased. The order typically is: spouse, children, parents, brothers and sisters, grandchildren, and great-grandchildren. The names of all these survivors except the grandchildren and great-grandchildren are generally reported. Only the number of grandchildren and great-grandchildren is included. In some families a listing of all their names could take up much of a column if they were reported. If only one or two relatives are still alive, you might report that information this way: Miss Smith is survived by her brother, Dennis Smith of New York.

The final section is devoted to funeral arrangements. It reports on the day and the hour of the service as well as the name of the funeral home so those wanting to attend can find it. The place of burial and the name of the minister are also included. Remember, when you are reporting on clergy members, the style of most newspapers calls for using "the Rev.," not just "Rev.," before their names, as in "the Rev. Elizabeth Milton."

If the family is requesting that contributions be made to a certain charity, you can include that at the end of the obituary. Some papers will precede it by saying "in lieu of flowers, the family asks that. . . ." Others, in deference to the florist who may be among their advertisers, elect not to use that phrase.

Often, because of the timing of the death, funeral arrangements may not yet have been completed. If so, report that funeral arrangements were incomplete at press time. The next day your editor will probably want you to write a second story on the death providing the information that was not yet ready in time for the first story.

Word Usage

Be careful with the usage of some words that might come up in the obituary. Do not report that someone died "of heart failure" because everyone who dies experiences heart failure. Do not say that someone died "from an operation" but rather "during an operation." It will make the surgeon happier. In the case of accidents, someone dies of injuries "suffered," not "received." Report that someone died "of" a disease, not "from" it.

Out of courtesy for the deceased, many papers will precede the last name of the individual who died with the courtesy title, "Mr.," in second reference, even if that is not the style throughout the rest of the paper.

Because of the harshness of referring to someone as a "widow" or "widower" so soon after a spouse's death, that surviving spouse is typically still referred to as a "wife" or "husband" in the obituary.

Do not use the more formal term, "interment," but rather "burial." If necessary to talk about the body, use that word and not "corpse," "dead body," or "remains." Use the simple word "die" and not "pass away," "expire," or "lose one's life."

Some papers have a general policy against reporting that death was the result of suicide. Their attitude is that this kind of personal emotional distress is not the sort of information that needs to be publicly aired. Exceptions are generally made, however, for celebrities and other newsworthy figures.

In cases where death was the result of unnatural causes, a coroner or other person in authority should be questioned about the cause and cited as the source of the information.

Watch Out for the Newsworthy

Be suspicious when reporting on deaths. Sometimes the death may not be as innocent as a routine funeral home form indicates. The story is told that late one Saturday night, just before the Sunday edition was to go to press, a stringer for a New York state paper called up to dictate three obituaries. Fortunately the reporter who happened to be taking the dictation was one of the paper's most skillful journalists. He became suspicious as to why these three individuals should all suddenly have died so late on a Saturday night. It was unusual for the medium-sized paper to have so many obituaries at that hour. He questioned the stringer about it, only to find out that the deaths were a result of a triple ax murder.

That information should, of course, have been written up as a news story and not a formal obituary. Watch out for that kind of news. The death of someone at a very young age, for instance, might raise some questions.

Another stringer, then responsible for coverage around Niagara Falls, Ontario, rightfully decided further questions had to be asked police about the circumstances of the death of someone found in the bottom of the Welland Canal. He was discovered with his hands handcuffed together behind his back and a concrete block tied to his feet. No foul play was suspected, police said. Often further questions need to be asked.

Sometimes the deceased deserve more information in their obituaries than can be obtained from a standard form. Look at past newspaper stories about them and question relatives, friends, and business associates. Make the reporting of their death come alive with fascinating facts.

Final tributes to the life of important contributors to our society can in the hands of skillful writers be among the best written pieces of the paper. Former *TV Guide* publisher, William Annenberg, the wealthy friend of Richard Nixon and at one time ambassador to Great Britain, thought obituaries could make such interesting reading that they might be the subject of a whole magazine. The magazine was to be called *Footprints* and cater to the kind of public craving for news of celebrities that made *People* magazine so very successful. The magazine never was published, but many newspapers realize the value of such celebrity obituaries.

For many years at *The New York Times* it was Alden Whitman, known during his reign as journalism's premier writer of obituaries, who was charged with interviewing the greats around the world in preparation for their death.

Writing in the journalism magazine *More,* he (1977) described those about whom it was especially a pleasure to say a final word. Among them were "Picasso, because he symbolized unfettered artistic genius; Bertrand Russell, because he dared to envision a better, more rational humanity; . . . Helen Keller, because she overcame; J. Robert Oppenheimer, because he had a sense of sin about the atomic bomb; . . . Haile Selassie, because he spit in Mussolini's eye in 1936; Earl Warren, because he had faith in the essential fairness of the American people. . . . But they were all interesting to do," he wrote, "because obits constitute part of the cultural continuum by which one generation carries on from another" (p. 15).

FEATURE ATTRACTIONS

If writing an effective hard news story in an inverted pyramid format is like constructing a good, solid building, writing an effective feature might instead be compared to staging a lively performance. To the solid substance of the basic structure must be added the flair, the style, the zip of an entertaining creation.

When to Use Features

What exactly is a feature? Journalism textbook writers have been struggling with the answer to that question. Here's how some of them have defined it.

Warren K. Agee, Phillip H. Ault, and Edwin Emery (1983), *Reporting and Writing the News*: "A story written with a 'soft' or nonspot news approach" (p. 372).

Judith L. Burken (1979), *Introduction To Reporting*: "Usually a non-dated story with human-interest angle in which only one side of a story or issue is presented. Also called soft news" (p. 209).

George A. Hough 3rd (1984), *News Writing*: "A type of news story, sometimes called a news feature. It is usually not breaking news, but a story closely related to news. Features are often interpretative, give background, play up human interest and convey the color of an event" (p. 415).

In short, it is hard to define—but you will know it when you see it.

I prefer to use the word "feature" for a certain style rather than a particular type of story subject because even breaking news can be featurized. You will have to judge on a case-by-case basis, at first perhaps with the help of your editor, whether a feature style is appropriate for the story you are writing.

When it is important that the reader know the factual aspects of the story in a direct and fast-reading manner, it is hard to beat the tried-and-true inverted pyramid form.

But if, for instance, the basic news about an event has already been reported and you want to provide related information, like a description of the people involved, a feature style can help you do that in what can be a more enticing, entertaining, or dramatic way.

Be careful not to use the feature style just to show off your creative writing abilities when an inverted pyramid style might be better. But do use it in cases where it will work well to give more impact to your story.

Feature Leads

Because the appropriate form varies depending on the subject, it is difficult to generalize about how best to write a feature. But one difference between the feature and inverted pyramid story is that the feature lead may be longer than that of the straight news story, continuing on in many cases for several paragraphs. Like the rest of the story, the feature lead needs to have a special zip to it, often drawing on techniques of some of the good fiction writers.

Experimentation and creativity are important in developing an effective feature style. As the form allows for a lot of flexibility, try out a large variety of leads.

Here are some suggestions for possible types of leads. Do not feel limited by them. There are many additional fine types of leads that will work well. But these may give you some ideas.

Quotation

If you have an exact quotation that works well in setting the tone for the story, go ahead and use it in your lead. But do not use a quote just to take the easy way out and borrow someone else's words. To work well, the quote has to set the right tone and focus, and it has to be worded directly enough and not wander. Especially be on the lookout for short, eye-catching quotes such as this one.

"I still," she muses, rapping her bony fingers against her graying head, "more or less have my what they call marbles," and she pulls her flowered shawl around

her a little closer, throws her head back and laughs gleefully. Alice Roosevelt
Longworth is 90 years old today. (Story by Sally Quinn in *The Washington Post*)

Description

The descriptive lead can offer an ideal way to set the tone of the story. Seek out
colorful details and paint a word picture of an event, an individual, a place.
Here's an example of a lead describing an event.

A solemn-faced man stands before a podium, a white cowboy hat set back on his
head. A standing-room-only crowd is silent as he recites in a deep, steady voice:
  Her feet were sharp, flanks were high, horns grew long and keen.
  She had all the lines, both blood and build, to be a wild cow queen.
  Several verses follow, elaborating on and exalting the life of this cow. This is
cowboy poetry, and this piece just one of the hundreds heard here at the first-
ever convention honoring this literary genre. (Story by Carrie Dolan in *The Wall
Street Journal*)

An example of a lead describing a person tops off this profile on the new
mayor of Portland, Oregon.

The full-bearded, barrel-chested man in the deerstalker cap shrugs out of his red-
checked Mackinaw and hitches up his knickers, ignoring his drooping left sock.
  The man is Bud Clark, who at the age of 54, is the new mayor of Portland.
(Story by Wallace Turner in *The New York Times*)

Notice how important the small details are at making these leads a success.
Even the kind of head attire can make a valuable contribution. Descriptions
like "a white cowboy hat set back on his head" and "full-bearded, barrel-chested
man in the deerstalker cap" are very revealing.
  The effective details in this lead describing a place may hit painfully close to
home.

This stately old Victorian house would make a stately old Victorian squirm.
  Dust coats the classics on the living-room bookcase and combines with dog hair
to form soft curls that ride the drafts in the hardwood hallway upstairs. Light
switches are mottled with fingerprints. In the dining room, the silver tea set has
turned golden.
  The lady of this particular house is a lawyer. "She raised five kids and got
burned out on housework and now has better things to do," says Brenda Bell,
digging away with a mop at some stubborn wax buildup in a kitchen corner. (Story
by Betsy Morris in *The Wall Street Journal*)

Contrast

Sometimes contrasting elements can help give impact to the lead.

Assigned to cover a triple murder and suicide on what otherwise was a tranquil Good Friday, I was struck by that contrast as well as the irony that the murder of the family happened on a family holiday marking the death of Christ. In the lead below I tried to work those elements into the lead for the story I wrote as a stringer for *The Milwaukee Journal*.

> It was Good Friday. Some filed to church to commemorate the death of Christ. Some used their holiday hours to spend time with their families.
>
> Oshkosh police officer Warrick Schroeder had requested the day off to attend a hearing on his divorce proceedings.
>
> But before the day was out, the Oshkosh man had fatally shot his estranged wife and their two children, then committed suicide with the same .357-caliber Magnum service revolver, according to information from eyewitnesses pieced together by police.

Indeed this was a hard news story, but I thought the feature lead worked best to get at the drama of this terrible family tragedy. The editors apparently agreed because they left the feature lead and ran the story on the front page.

In addition to providing impact, contrast can help explain the situation and give perspective. Take this example on the rise and fall of garbanzos.

> Just as the garbanzo is becoming a staple of restaurant salad bars and home salad mixing, California garbanzo production is collapsing. (Story by Eric Brazil in *USA Today*)

Comparison

Comparing the subject of a lead with something else can also help give impact. A simile makes that comparison with the use of "like" or "as," and a metaphor does it without those words.

The following lead makes use of a simile.

> Hans Hofsehroer raced like a stallion across the showroom and shook Sally Morse's hand.
>
> "I can't believe I got him," said Morse, who had just ponied up $13,000 to buy Tacino, a gray, 4-year-old Oldenburg gelding that Hofsehroer bought in Germany 10 months ago. (Story by Lawrence Shulruff in *The Denver Post*)

Alliteration

Sometimes another literary device, alliteration, in which the writer repeats the same consonant sound at the beginning of nearby words, can give just the right special effect.

USA Today used this device in the first paragraph of its story reporting on media mogul Ted Turner:

> Ted Turner is taking on Tinseltown.
>   Having scored an impressive assault on the big three TV networks with his highly acclaimed, but financially strapped, Cable News Network and his money-making "Superstation" WTBS, the brash TV entrepreneur says he is "close" to an agreement with Hollywood producer Ray Stark to make feature films. (Story by Mark Field in *USA Today*)

Alliteration can be especially effective in creating a humorous or breezy tone or in establishing a lyrical, poetic mood.

Listing

Leading with a list of specifics can be another feature approach. For instance:

> There was a snowman in front of the Alamo, people went skiing under palm trees, garages collapsed and the city of San Antonio, which does not own a snowplow, had to shut its doors completely today in the wake of a snowstorm even Chicago could not have ignored. (Story by Wayne King in *The New York Times*)

In collecting your list, try to pick especially colorful examples and ones that help set the right tone, as these do in describing San Antonio's plight.

Parody

You might want to try drawing from familiar phrases such as those in proverbs, songs, book titles, well-known quotations, advertisements, and common sayings, as in the following lead.

> Neither rain nor paranoia nor fear of terrorist attack can keep the Cannes Film Festival from its appointed hysteria. (Story by Jack Curry in *USA Today*)

Follow-Up

To emphasize what has happened over the passage of time, use a lead that focuses on the past and compares it with the current situation.

> As teen-agers in the late 1960s, Charles Walker and Olin Smith worked side by side in a chemical plant here, dumping barrels of brownish powder into huge vats and then cleaning up the grime and dust after the chemical reaction produced textile dyes.
>
> Workers griped among themselves about conditions in the dusty mixing room that they called "the hole." But it was not until last week, more than 15 years later, that Walker and Smith, now in their 30s, said they learned from a television news report that the chemical powder was beta-naphthyalamine (BNA) and that it can cause cancer and related disorders. (Story by Peter Perl in *The Washington Post*)

Historical Allusion

This lead makes a reference to some well-known event or individual in history. To work, the reference must be familiar to readers.

Because even younger readers know who Frank Sinatra is, the following lead's allusion is effective.

> Not since Frank Sinatra was a bobby-soxer idol has socks appeal been mentioned in the same breath with sex appeal. (Story by Bettijane Levine in the *Los Angeles Times*)

Direct Address

This lead addresses the readers directly, as if the writer were engaging in conversation with them. The pronoun "you" helps create that feeling. It is a very casual type of lead and can be especially effective in self-help articles. Take this example:

> If you're still confused about how to choose among the dozens of long-distance telephone carriers spawned by the breakup of AT&T, a computer analysis of your monthly bill may be the answer. (Story by Joe Krakoviak in *USA Today*)

Question

This lead, too, is usually best used for a story with a more casual approach. The risk is that it can be overused. Save it for when it really works well, as in this lead.

Can Don Johnson of Miami gun down the Ewings of Dallas?

We'll find out this fall when NBC's "Miami Vice" moves to 9 p.m. Friday to go head-to-head in a ratings war with CBS' "Dallas." (Story by Monica Collins in *USA Today*)

Analysis

Better check with your editor before you try out this lead. It may not be viewed as acceptable for the section for which you are writing. Some editors will not permit this type of lead at all, and others will only allow it to be used by their most experienced reporters, writing about topics on which they have special expertise. It attempts to put the news event into perspective for the reader instead of just reporting on it.

President Reagan's budget, an aggressive assault on a wide range of popular spending programs, represents his administration's best and perhaps last chance to shrink the size of government. (Story by Paul Blustein and Laurie McGinley in *The Wall Street Journal*)

Staccato

This short, choppy form can be effectively used to create a mood of excitement, speed, or suspense. Here it is used to contribute a feeling of excitement and tension as the author describes a raging battle.

Catherine Tankoos and James Miles are at war.

It will last only an hour or so, and they will be friends when it's over. But for now, the two prominent Palm Beachers are enemies. Under a relentless Florida sun, they stalk each other, heavy wooden mallets in hand and looking to exploit any weakness. They will strike mercilessly, if they find one.

They're playing croquet. Yes, croquet. But this is championship croquet. Often viciously competitive, it couldn't easily be confused with the casual backyard game in which most of the balls end up in the bushes. (Story by Jeffrey Lincoln in *The Wall Street Journal*)

Suspense

Keep the readers guessing with this lead. By preserving the suspense, you will keep them reading, as in this example.

Almost overnight, a renewed interest in sex education was displayed in this quiet, unpretentious San Diego County community.

Little wonder.

One of the counselors at the town's only high school reported that 20 percent of the school's girls admitted to her that they were pregnant during the 1983-84 school year. A disproportionately large number were freshmen. (Story by Tom Gorman in the *Los Angeles Times*)

Anecdote

If you have an anecdote that is appropriate to help set the focus, it can make a terrific lead, as in the following example.

Judi Wright didn't pay attention Friday afternoon when her daughter Jennifer came to her in their Surrey Ridge home and told her: "Mom, there is a big storm over there."

"I just ignored her," Mrs. Wright said.

Then the tornado hit Surrey Ridge. (Story by Bill McBean in *The Denver Post*)

Playing With Words

Sometimes playing around with words can give you the kind of lift you need for your story. For instance:

Fast food is on a fast track in downtown Minneapolis. (Story by Paul Klauda in the *Minneapolis Star and Tribune*)

Or how about this pun in a story about a search for ancient bones?

For Mary Romig, work is the pits—and she loves it.

Specifically her labor of love is at the bottom of a stinky 13-foot-deep black hole called Pit 91. (Story by Jerry Belcher in the *Los Angeles Times*)

Combining Style and Substance

Openers such as these will help arouse the reader's interest. The lead of a feature is an attention-grabber, just like the first number in a performance. But once it captures the attention, the rest of the story must hold it. The feature must be an effective combination of good style and substance.

After the lead, or opener as it is often known in feature writing, comes the bridge into the main body of the story. The bridge helps to emphasize the basic substance or focus of the story. If you are having trouble making the bridge work, it may be due to the fact that the lead was chosen just because it was colorful or entertaining and does not get at the right substance. With the right lead, the bridge can work smoothly as a transition into the remainder of the story.

To have impact, the story needs effective focus and organization. Material extraneous to the substance of the story must be tossed, even if it was gathered with great expense of time. Sometimes as the reporter is in the process of rounding up material, it is impossible to tell what will prove to be useful and what will have to be discarded. Remember that more is not necessarily better. Get rid of information that tends to distract from the story.

Webster's definitions for the word "feature" include "a distinct or outstanding part or quality of something" and "a special attraction." Keep uppermost in mind that distinct quality or special attraction of what you are shining the spotlight on as you write your feature.

And keep your audience in mind as your piece unfolds. Features are generally considerably longer than regular hard news stories, yet you have to try to sustain interest throughout.

What tricks of the trade are available to help maintain interest? Using specific examples, especially individual human examples with generous amounts of colorful quotes, can be a lively device. And revealing anecdotes appropriate for the focus of the story are the expert feature writer's treasure. Collect them wherever you can find them.

The DEE Formula

A frequently used format for arranging information in a feature story has come to be known as the DEE (description, explanation, evaluation) formula. Often associated with *The Wall Street Journal*, which uses it frequently, this format begins with a specific, detailed description—perhaps of a person, an event, or a place.

In the next part of the story that example described in the opener is put in context and explained. Often the explanation is that the information in the lead is representative of many other individuals sharing a similar problem or is part of a trend.

The last portion, the evaluation section, includes opinions of individuals asked to comment on the phenomenon outlined in the explanation section.

In this example, written by James S. Hirsch, the opening of *The Wall Street Journal* piece used the format, beginning with an example of a stressed-out employee's "need to be kneaded":

> Debora Foster takes off her necklace, settles herself on a padded chair and gently leans forward. With a jazz-piano tape playing softly in the background, the soothing hands of Sabina Vidunas begin to work on Ms. Foster's neck and shoulders.

"It's like an oasis in this room," Ms. Foster purrs. The room in question is the directors' lounge of H. J. Heinz Co., 60 floors above the bustle of Pittsburgh. There, amid oil paintings and marble tables, massages are administered every Wednesday.

The example about Ms. Foster is followed by an explanation about the trend, which the *Journal* reports is "infiltrating corporate America." Usually in specially designed chairs in dimly lighted conference rooms, Hirsh writes, fully clothed stressed-out employees enjoy 15-minute massage sessions.

Later, in the evaluation section, individuals comment on the phenomenon. Massage advocates cite positive effects, including easing of tension and improvement of morale. Others describe problems with negative images associated with massage. The opinion of one purist, who thinks clothes take away from the experience, was reserved for the ending: "There's nothing like skin to skin."

By leading off with the example of the H. J. Heinz employee, the writer has turned the piece on the new trend for relieving corporate stress into a story with human impact. It is a typical example of the way in which the *Journal* has managed to make an unlikely subject, financial news, among the most readable stories in papers today. And that flair is no doubt largely responsible for the *Journal*'s huge success—it now boasts more paid individual subscribers than any other U.S. daily newspaper.

But at the same time that it uses this stylish device to capture our attention, the *Journal* provides the facts and figures and expert opinions to help us thoroughly understand and evaluate the phenomenon. The feature attraction is not just entertaining. It is full of useful information.

Color Stories

One of the special attractions that a feature can provide so well is a description of an event that allows readers to feel as if they are there experiencing the happening.

It is known as a color story because of the vivid description that gives the reader a sense of the color of the event.

In the hands of a skilled writer it looks so easy. Often the subject matter is not deep and ponderous but rather light and fun. But the apparent simplicity and easygoing style of a good color story come only after a time-consuming job of collecting the many details that will make the story work.

Done right, the effective color story will take the readers to the scene and allow them to sense the goings-on even though they were unable to have been physically present themselves. But it can also prove good reading for those who were in attendance. It can help them appreciate what they experienced and add background information about which they might have been unaware.

Your editor may assign you to cover an event in your community that is expected to attract a lot of interest but involves little in the way of real newsy information you can grasp hold of and report. For instance, perhaps you are asked to cover a tractor-pulling contest, a greased-pig-catching competition, a broomball tournament, an ice-sculpture contest, a bathtub race, or an outdoor art fair. Your solution: Write a color story using an effective feature style.

Remember, no matter how effective your writing style, you are not likely to make it work right if you have not first been a diligent collector of the small details that will give the needed color to your story. Be sure to set aside enough time for the task. You may be surprised to find it could take a half a day just to assemble the bits and pieces.

In accomplishing this task, you will have to use all of your senses and be an especially alert observer. Do not trust your memory. Record in your notebook every possible usable detail. You can select the ones you need when writing up your story. This is not the kind of story that you can put together after the event is over by questioning someone who was there. You must be there yourself— and you must be an active observer.

For instance, if you are covering Hometown's annual Great Bathtub Race, examine the strange craft carefully before the race. Jot down some of the colorful names the bathtubs have been dubbed. Note the various types of tubs with information on their colors and shapes.

Watch and record how their owners are preparing their vessels for the race. And when the race begins, observe not just the competitors but also the spectators.

Listen for the instructions of the officials and the call to start the race.

Describe the race itself, with all of its frustrations and victories. Remember that you want to bring the scene to the reader who was unable to attend.

But in addition to being a keen observer, you will also have to spend some time interviewing individuals to provide the necessary background information.

Find out, for instance, how the event happened to get started in the community, whether interest has grown, what requirements the tubs must meet, to what the winner attributes success, and what preparation was involved in getting ready for the race.

You are likely to get all sorts of unexpected and colorful quotes from the zany sportsters who compete in such a meet.

Mingle their quotes together with the details you have observed and you should have a story that will be very readable even for those who were right alongside you watching the tubs skim through the water.

Look how a color story can work in the hands of a master. Let's analyze this story from The Associated Press. Paragraphs have been numbered to facilitate reference to them in the analysis that follows.

1. From the tip of his elongated snout to the end of his ratlike tail, Barbecue Wennichverlieren looked every inch the magnificent thoroughbred, born to run.

2. On Sunday, at the call to the post—"Gentlemen, start your 'dillos" —he clawed eagerly at the sun baked track. His humped, hinged, armor plated shell and stubby legs quivered with anticipation.

3. The track was fast. All bets were down. Excitement rippled through the crowd jamming the grandstand at the Gillespie County Fairgrounds.

4. And at the crack of the starter's rifle, Barbecue was off, churning, swaying and hopping in the fashion of a true thoroughbred armadillo.

5. It takes only a few moments for a good 'dillo to cover the 15 yards or so that make a racecourse, and the finishes are often close. Barbecue was in it all the way, but he was second—by a snout—to a speedster by the name of Hill Country Holler No. 7.

6. And in the Texas Invitational Armadillo Races, second doesn't count for much. Especially in this German settled part of Texas, where people know the loser's name translates to "Barbecue If I Lose."

7. Until a few years ago, the armadillo—a docile, burrowing mammal about the size of an overfed house cat and covered with a bony but pliable crescent shaped shell—was most often seen mashed on the highway.

8. But the odd looking creature became the symbol of progressive country music—country influenced by rock—and where the music was popular, suddenly armadillos were popular. For every weekend of this summer, there is an armadillo race in southern or central Texas.

9. It's all quite informal. Hill Country Holler No. 7's trainers are regulars on the racing circuit, and they had caught the winner—plus Hill Country Holler Nos. 8, 9, 10 and 11—on Saturday.

10. "We go out and catch 10 or 11 the day before the race," said Steve Fraunhofer, holding the champion aloft by its tail. "We try to sneak up on them, but that usually doesn't work. So we just chase them down. Then we pick the five feistiest ones, the ones that try to tear out of the sacks.

11. "If we get a good one, we keep him for maybe two races. They start getting too tame after that. If they don't run good, we either let them go or barbecue and eat 'em," he added.

12. Training methods differ. The champion had been transported in a customized box, while Barbecue Wennichverlieren arrived in the bottom of a burlap sack after being stabled overnight in a large trash can.

13. Go-Getter and Sue came in the arms of their trainers, with Lone Star Beer stickers slapped on their shells.

14. The racing rules take into account that armadillos rarely run in a straight line. The race starts with the 'dillos facing out from a tight circle, each held by the tail. At the start, they are released into the larger circle that surrounds the small one. The winner is the first one out of the large circle.

15. Dr. Frank Weaker, a San Antonio veterinarian, was on hand to make sure the armadillos were treated humanely and hadn't been drugged.

16. He also checked to make sure they were thoroughbreds. Veteran racers like to tell about the time someone tried to enter a jackrabbit wearing a football helmet.

The writer has chosen to use an extended metaphor to help add a whimsical tone to the description of this silly race. By comparing the competition of the armadillos to a thoroughbred horse race, the fashioner of the color story adds to the subtly humorous tone that permeates the piece. And so, in the first paragraph, "Barbecue Wennichverlieren looked every inch the magnificent thoroughbred, born to run." The absurd name of the second-place contender is worked right into the first paragraph to capitalize on its humor.

Notice how effectively a precise description of the critter is worked into the story. The first paragraph tells of "his elongated snout" and "ratlike tail." The second paragraph describes his "humped, hinged, armor plated shell and stubby legs" drawing upon alliteration to help create a humorous tone.

Later, in Paragraph 7, the description continues so effectively that even if we previously had no idea of what an armadillo looked like, we do now. It is described as "a docile, burrowing mammal about the size of an overfed house cat and covered with a bony but pliable crescent shaped shell."

But back to the second paragraph. Notice the exact words of the race starter, "Gentlemen, start your 'dillos." It's followed by a great description of the dillo's reaction using colorful verbs and adjectives. He "clawed eagerly at the sun baked track" and his "stubby legs quivered with anticipation."

The sense of excitement created in that sentence is effectively continued in the next paragraph, with its short, choppy sentences that give a feel of fast-paced action: "The track was fast. All bets were down." And then a longer sentence with a change of pace and additional colorful verbs: "Excitement rippled through the crowd jamming the grandstand at the Gillespie County Fairgrounds."

You do need to work in the straightforward details like the place of the event, but try to do it unobtrusively, as the writer does in this third paragraph.

The next paragraph, like the sixth and eighth, illustrates why you should forget any rules you might have learned in English class about never beginning a paragraph with "and" or "but." Although that is a good rule to follow for more formal writing, in a light feature such as this, they can add a nice flow to the description.

Look at the great use of verbs in that fourth paragraph. "Barbecue was off, churning, swaying and hopping" and then, getting back to the racetrack metaphor, "in the fashion of a true thoroughbred armadillo."

Using dashes in a light feature can also give an effective pacing, as demonstrated in the fifth, as well as the second, seventh, eighth, and ninth paragraphs.

In the sixth paragraph the writer starts to give us the information that helps us understand the cultural background of the race—and the reason for Barbecue Wennichverlieren's name. The backgrounding continues through the eighth paragraph and is an illustration of the kind of information that must be collected through interviews.

Interviewing must also have been the source of the information about the selection of the racers, which starts in the ninth paragraph, with the effective transition, "It's all quite informal." The lack of discriminating selection is subtly documented in Paragraph 9 with "they had caught the winner—plus Hill Country Holler Nos. 8, 9, 10 and 11—on Saturday."

Recognizing the value of good quotes, the writer lets the trainer speak on at length in Paragraphs 10 and 11.

Notice how a description of the speaker is colorfully interjected between the quotes in Paragraph 10 with the words, "holding the champion aloft by its tail."

With the short and effective bridge, "Training methods differ," Paragraph 12 gets into those methods. A description of how he had been "stabled overnight in a large trash can" again gets us back to the thoroughbred racehorse metaphor.

Again in the Paragraph 13 alliteration is used effectively—"with Lone Star Beer stickers slapped on their shells."

Paragraph 14 explains the rules of the race, whereas Paragraph 15 sets us up for the anecdote that was such an effective ending for the piece:

"He also checked to make sure they were thoroughbreds. (The ending concludes with a continuation of the extended horse-racing metaphor and thus nicely relates back to the opening.) Veteran racers like to tell about the time someone tried to enter a jackrabbit wearing a football helmet."

Unlike a story written in the inverted pyramid format, which can just sort of trail away with the least important information last, a feature story needs an effective ending. Good writers often save effective quotes or anecdotes for the ending and are especially on the lookout for ones that share the tone and focus for the rest of the story and give a final kind of feeling to the end. Be careful to avoid the shortcomings of inexperienced writers who use the ending for a judgmental, subjective statement or to repeat information they wish to emphasize but that has already been reported earlier.

Before you start writing your feature, think how you will leave your audience. If it is a humorous piece you plan to write, you might want to try to leave them chuckling. But if it is an inspirational piece, for instance, quite a different ending would be appropriate.

Your aim, unlike in inverted pyramid stories, is not to come up with the most cuttable information for your ending. Although it is likely your story may have to be cut, good editors will try to preserve your ending and cut from within. Because feature stories are usually less timely than many written in an inverted pyramid style, the notion is that editors will not generally be rushed into making fast cuts in features.

Profiles

These various writing suggestions can also be applied to the feature interview or personality profile that is used so often in newspapers today.

We examined earlier how to conduct an interview. In writing up the information gathered from that interview for a personality profile, decide what characteristic you would like to stress and focus your story around it. The process is similar to that of an artist selecting a distinguishing trait or two to use in drawing a caricature of the individual. A political cartoonist portraying Ronald Reagan might stress his hair, drawing Jimmy Carter might focus on the toothy grin, and sketching Richard Nixon might emphasize the jowls.

Describing a successful businessman? Perhaps the best focus may be on his life as a workaholic—or his contributions to the community—or his willingness to take risks. Use that main trait as the core of your story and assemble your information around it.

Be careful that the profile does not just read like a cut-and-dry extended resume. Borrow from the techniques of the short-story writer to give it life. Unobtrusively work the necessary details, such as a person's age, into the flow of the story. And weave in physical descriptions of the individuals, their gestures, and surroundings.

Through your personality profiles you are trying to get inside the skin of your subjects and see what makes them tick. It can be very difficult to do even for someone you know well. It is really a challenge for someone you never met before.

Be careful to capture the complexities of individuals. Some of the most fascinating people exhibit traits which seem almost contradictory. Perhaps some of Elvis Presley's appeal, for instance, was the mixed portrait of the tough-appearing rock 'n' roller and the kindly celebrity who generously gave away expensive presents to associates and starred in many movie roles as Hollywood's Mr. Nice Guy. And then there's the blond and buxom sweet-voiced Dolly Parton whose interview story revealed an intelligent, determined, creative songwriter.

Tell about the inner thinkings of your subject as well as their deeds. Readers like to live vicariously and share the lives of the rich, the famous, the creative, the powerful. And they learn from the experiences of others—their mistakes as well as their successes.

Everyone is in need of heroes and role models to inspire and lead. We need to inspire with our profiles but at the same time we must report the human frailties and shortcomings. And in some cases those human foibles make the lives of the successful more inspiring. They are not, after all, so very different from the rest of us, the reader thinks, and look what they have managed to achieve.

The profile must breathe life into the subject, not sound like an obituary listing of the person's accomplishments. Generously intersperse direct quotes from the individual that give a flavor of the way he or she thinks as well as speaks. Add physical descriptions of clothes, hairstyle, gestures, or whatever else will help complete the portrait.

Here are suggestions magazine editor Don McKinney (1983) made on "How To Make Your Articles Sparkle" in his article written for *Writer's Digest* magazine:

> If you are writing a story about some living person, what has been known as a 'profile' ever since the *New Yorker* invented the term back in 1925, the most important thing you can do is make the person seem as alive to your readers as he or she seemed to you when you did the interview. This comes about largely through an accumulation of seemingly unimportant details, an accurate reproduction of the subject's way of speaking, and a series of anecdotes which reveal his or her character. (p. 30)

And describe their setting. It is likely to be a reflection of their attitude and interests. The lovingly tended garden, the piles of newspapers and magazines and well-stocked library, the drawings by children and crayoned walls, the racquets and fishing rods, statues and oil paintings—all can add color and insight to the story.

Be creative, Be flexible. Use whatever technique works. But remember, the feature story must answer the basic questions that might arise in the minds of the readers. Be careful that you do not get so involved with your creative writing that you forget to include all the needed facts.

Collect the details you will need, then organize and report them with your focus firmly in mind. Bind them all together with effective transitions and revel in the results. The resulting artistic creation should be a pleasing blend of style and substance.

STYLE AND PACING

The same information conveyed by different writers can have varying degrees of effectiveness, depending on the style of writing they use in relating it. Style as well as substance is important in good newswriting.

You have experienced how style of expression can make a difference in your daily life. The style used in giving an order to a child may be very important in determining whether that order will be obeyed. Similarly, the style you use in approaching the mayor with a request may help determine the response. So too in your writing. The style will help determine how effective your piece is.

Style as Personal Expression

What is involved in writing style? Here is the view of Everette E. Dennis and Arnold H. Ismach (1981) set forth in their journalism textbook, *Reporting Processes and Practices: Newswriting for Today's Readers*: "Style is the distinctive aspects of written expression, the manner of organization of material—the actual execution of words, sentences and paragraphs. A writing style is a form of personal expression developed by the individual" (p. 122).

And to a certain extent it may be an innate quality. That's the outlook of Paul Darcy Boles (1985). "It is, to some extent, born into its owner; for the rest, it is a result of individuality as firmly expressed as a fingerprint" (p. 24), he said in his article, "The Elements of Your Personal Writing Style," published in *Writer's Digest* magazine.

As an example of how individual style can affect the impact of a work, listen to the performance of "The Star-Spangled Banner" in the hands of various singers at sporting events. Each brings to it his or her own unique style, and the effect is altered.

That type of personal expression shows up in the way people dress, decorate their homes, speak and, of course, use their artistic talents.

Hiley H. Ward (1985), in his textbook, *Professional Newswriting,* said editors look for "the enigmatic sense of style which is to writing as charisma is to personality" (p. 174).

The writer's personal view helps shape that style. Ward said:

> One ingredient which affects both the techniques of a style and also the general tone and organization involved in writing with style is how the writer looks at life. This personal view is the beginning of all style. What color are the writer's inner eyeglasses to the world? . . .
>
> If the writer views the world with creativity and curiosity and with some kind of organizing principle—a philosophy or even a method of searching—the writer stands on the ground of style. If the writer is boring inwardly . . . this person will lack style. Unless some character trait or guiding light or commitment to ideas, including a commitment to the human race—some kind of altruistic principle beyond ego and self-preservation—energizes the writer, the hope for style in this person's writing is distant indeed. (pp. 174, 175)

The Development of Style

Style seems often to evolve and be strengthened as the writer grows and matures. Yet even with years of practice, few writers really achieve the ability to write with exceptional style. According to Ward, "At most newspapers, one—maybe two—journalists are known for writing with style. Their ranks are thin; many covet to write like them, but few achieve it" (p. 203).

Generally it is a good idea for beginning writers to stick with a more straightforward style. Frequently, only after years of news writing, do more distinctive styles evolve effectively.

Often that evolution involves a lot of trial and error and falling short. Here's how journalist Gary Metro (1981) experimented with developing his style, according to his description of his efforts in a column written for the *Weekend Northwestern* newspaper published in Oshkosh, Wisconsin.

> Starting out as a writer is a lot like trying on new clothing. A person can find a multitude of styles to choose from and some of the selections have certain attractive features. You like flash? No problem. How about something elegant and flowing? It's in stock. . . .

I've been at this writing thing for quite some time. It's given me a chance to look at a different style or two.

There was a time that I started fooling around with unbelievably long sentences which would start at one end of the idea spectrum and move ever so slowly, like molasses on a frigid January morning deep in the heart of snow-encrusted Alaska, I mean Alaska for goodness sake, that by the time the subject of the sentence came shooting by again the reader was just never exactly certain of what was supposed to be going on, anyhow, if you know what I mean, without having to draw a little picture or some durn fool thing like that there. . . .

A few years back, one of the raging gimmicks could be found most commonly in novels. . . . It had an air of excitement about it and certainly attracted a lot of attention, but it never lasted a full season.

Maybe. You. Remember. The. One. Word. Sentence? Sure. It. Has. Impact. But. It. Grows. Tedious. . . .

Anyhow, most writers fool around with a lot of stuff like this until they try something which feels so comfortable that the words keep flowing without conscious thought. (p. A-7)

Eventually you are likely to find the form of personal expression that is most comfortable for you.

Novelist John Updike compared the process of writing with that of becoming a musician. First musicians learn to identify and play individual notes and to read music. They practice playing scales and perform simple compositions. Only after they master the fundamentals can they begin to develop their own manner of musical expression, their own style. Writers too must first master the basics, learn the craft of writing, and then explore further.

They must remember that style has little to do with ostentation in language. It is not fancy tricks and ornamentation—flashiness can stand in the way of coherent thought. There is a fine line between writing a stylish story that fits the content well and just showboating—so be careful, yet willing to experiment.

"Many reporters stumble along on a plateau of monotony in their writing because they do not make the necessary effort to improve their style," said Warren K. Agee, Phillip H. Ault, and Edwin Emery (1983) in their book, *Reporting and Writing the News*. "Others, exhilarated by the heady wine of words, succumb to the sin of 'fancy writing' that besets those who strain too hard for effect. Successful writing is never pompous or overstated" (p. 114).

Substance Helps Determine Style

Your style of writing should vary from story to story, depending on the substance about which you are writing. Appropriateness is a crucial concern for a successful blend of style and substance. The tone must be appropriate to the substance.

Just as the writer must think carefully about the total story and where it is headed before composing a lead, so too must he or she take that forward look in deciding what style to use, how to express the information.

It is the same kind of concern for appropriateness that we consciously or unconsciously consider when coming up with our own style of dress and evaluating that of others. The student who comes to class in blue jeans and a sweater is thought to be dressing appropriately for that class, but if the student were to show up in the same outfit for a night at the symphony, heads might turn.

And if the student arriving for class in that outfit added a pair of beautiful, expensive diamond earrings, some might question the tastefulness of the attire, no matter how valuable the jewelry.

Stylish individuals tend to dress with a certain image in mind. They may be attempting to project a professional, classic look, or perhaps their look is more exotic and glamorous or artsy and colorful. And that look may change depending on the occasion. But no matter what the look, each item selected helps in projecting the sought-after appearance. They have given some thought to the kind of statement they wish to make and know what to add to help make that statement.

Similar forethought is given to the decoration of a home. Perhaps the look may be contemporary, country, French provincial, or early student. But the look that tends to work best is one with a certain effect in mind and with objects that all help to create that effect.

Introducing an item with a different tone can detract from that look. Take, for instance, the living room furnished with an early student atmosphere. Filing cabinets topped off by a door are used for a desk, crates serve as bookshelves, and discarded items from the folks' attic complete the scene. Then a new sofa fresh from the store is added to the mix. Suddenly the rest of the furnishings can look drab and decrepit when before they had just seemed interesting. And the new cherished sofa just sticks out like a show dog amid waifs at the pound.

The writer, too, must have in mind what effect is desired and then use those writing techniques that will help accomplish that goal. A feature approach used for a subject that would more appropriately lend itself to a straight news format will undermine the story. Using a feature tone just because it is more showy and able to let you use creative flourishes is like wearing diamond earrings with a sporty outfit just because you want to show them off. It destroys the story like the earrings destroy the outfit.

On the other hand, if you are going to a fancy ball, you may want to add some jewelry to give some sparkle to your outfit. The pieces of jewelry can give it more impact, more flair. And so too, less straightforward writing is sometimes needed to add the necessary impact.

Think about what your main focus is and what you are trying to accomplish, then write your story accordingly with the appropriate manner of expression.

Should your story have a humorous tone, an aura of excitement? Does it

need to be flowing and lyrical or direct and straightforward? Adapt your tone
to fit the substance.

How to Alter Tone

Your selection of illustrations, quotes, and facts; your choice of words; the length
of your paragraphs and sentences—all help to establish the tone of your piece.
Look at how *St. Louis Post-Dispatch* writer Ronald J. Lawrence set the tone in
this story. He described the security measures that were being taken for the
trial of men who it was feared had made powerful, deadly enemies during three
years of gang warfare they were accused of starting.

> The security surrounding the Leisure gang trial begins each weekday morning
> with a ritual outside the Federal Courthouse downtown.
>   Between 8 and 9 a.m., several cars screech to a halt on the east side of the
> Courthouse. Well-dressed men jump out. With military precision, they take their
> positions. Some are armed with M-16s, automatic military rifles. They nervously
> scan the rooftops of nearby buildings.
>   Traffic on 11th Street is stopped. Pedestrians are halted by men with their rifles
> held rigidly across their chests.
>   Then another car stops at the curb. More armed men help underworld figure
> Paul J. Leisure out and put him into a wheelchair. Surrounded, he is wheeled up
> on a ramp and into the building. Parts of both of his legs were blown off when his
> car was bombed Aug. 11, 1981.

The no-nonsense military-like mood of the occasion is reflected in the short,
direct sentences describing the security measures. The specifics help to set the
scene, telling of the wary precaution surrounding the important trial. Verbs like
"screech," "jump," "armed," "scan," and "halt" further add to the mood.
    On the other hand, a story about a creatively artistic person might do better
with a more flowing tone. Take the way Laurie Horn described performance
artist Mary Luft in *The Miami Herald*.

> Back in 1979, the word about Mary Luft used to bubble through the Miami arts
> community like eerie chimes and light projections through the leaves in her old-
> Grovey back yard. . . .
>   To a small, self-selecting group of Miami arts fanatics, missing one of Mary's
> 'things' was tantamount to a football fan missing a playoff game. Even if you didn't
> like what might happen, you had to be there.
>   In her hauntingly lit yard, you might be pelted with bananas or over-whelmed
> by hordes of people stamping on a roof. At a Coral Gables gymnastic studio, you
> might sink serenely into an exercise mat as Luft sat behind a row of little chimes,

intoning the names of her close family and friends while slides of a little girl in Sioux City, Iowa, flashed behind her.

That was well before most in South Florida had learned the words "performance artist" or understood that Luft was becoming one.

No direct sentences with military-like precision in this piece. They meander and flow and sing. And they use literary devices. The simile in the first sentence compares the word about the artist to eerie chimes and light projections through leaves, and in the second paragraph an art fanatic missing Luft's performance is compared to a football fan missing a playoff game. The imaginative comparisons add sparkle to the piece.

Here the creative and flowing tone of the writing harmonizes with its artistic subject.

Does your story have a serious subject? Make sure the tone of your writing is appropriately serious. Don't, for instance, report on toxic-waste concerns aired at a board meeting by saying: "A report on problems with the proposed landfill site caused some raised eyebrows among county board members." The discussion on whether toxic wastes might leak out into neighboring wells is a deadly serious one that is not properly reported on by referring to raised eyebrows.

On the other hand, if the subject is a humorous one, use a light touch in reporting on it. Be careful. Humor can be surprisingly difficult to handle. If it misses the mark, it can really fall flat. A good choice of words, effective timing, and breezy sentences can be crucial.

The length of your sentences can do as much as your words to set the mood of your story. Shorter sentences can give it a lightness, a sense of movement, excitement. Long, flowing sentences can give a poetic or tranquil effect. They can also be appropriate for a more serious, somber tone.

Pacing

A mix of different lengths and types of sentences can help give movement, pacing to your piece.

That sense of pacing is important to develop, especially when you are writing a longer story. You want to keep the reader with you to the bitter end, if possible. You are writing to communicate with others, not just as therapy for yourself, and you cannot communicate with words that are not read.

Variety is important in creating effective pacing. Mix in quotations throughout. Avoid long sections of statistics—intersperse those figures at appropriate spots in the story. Weave in anecdotes and colorful details, when possible.

And toss out details that do not work to help your story. Are they important, intriguing, or in some other way contributors to the focus of your story? If not, out they go. Too many articles are ruined by insignificant detail.

Don't try to feed your readers garbage unrelated to the focus. As Melvin Mencher (1984) said in *News Reporting and Writing,* "The story should be like the meal set on the table, not the remnants in the sink. Everyone who sets words on paper for a living goes through the anxieties of cutting back, of discarding quotes, of tossing out details. Once the theme is set, cutting and discarding are essential" (p. 228).

But it is not an easy process, even after years of practice. Ernest Hemingway read 5 hours a day and wrote and rewrote as he learned to master his craft. He reportedly wrote the ending to *A Farewell to Arms* 39 times. And as a journalist covering the police court for *The Kansas City Star,* he would take his notes home and rework them for hours to simplify his writing until he had captured the essence of what he wanted to say in a few words.

Once you have found the tone and pacing that are appropriate to the story, the piece will have a vitality that makes it work. It is as if somewhere there was a form in which the story was meant to take shape, and you have found it and made it your own.

C H A P T E R ■ 1 6

TECHNICAL PROBLEMS

Editors grumble. Young writers today cannot write grammatically or spell correctly, they complain. An editor's valuable time is spent mopping up after the technical errors of others.

Perhaps the problem is, to a certain extent, being corrected as the nation's attention has been called to the inferior writing skills of many students and more effort is placed on overcoming the technical weaknesses. Yet, even the most professional of writers have shortcomings in need of correction. Even the most highly respected paper in the country, *The New York Times*, contains enough errors that they are accumulated regularly in its *Winners and Sinners* bulletin. And so too may you be guilty of some of the more common transgressions.

This chapter is designed to point out some of the most troublesome of the errors that seem to plague journalists. It does not attempt to serve as a grammar handbook. Many other books have been published to serve that purpose, and you might want to review one of them if you feel particularly in need of more extensive assistance. What it does do is remind you of some of the rules you may have forgotten and point out others that you perhaps have not run across.

In writing for print, we are expected to play by the rules of the game and break them only for special effect. Grammar is that set of rules we are expected to follow in combining words and punctuation into larger units. Because journalistic writing often has to be done under deadline pressure, the ability to churn out sentences within the rules of grammar without having to give it a second thought is crucial.

Here, then, are some reminders to help you do that.

Number Agreement

The basic rule to remember is that the verb must agree in number with the subject. But that rule is not always so easy to apply.

1. One common error is to become confused by phrases and clauses that come between the subject and predicate. Do not allow those words to cause you to lose sight of the subject.

> The pile of papers left by the
> students was blown away by the wind.
> ("Pile," a singular noun, is the subject.)

> The captain of the basketball team,
> as well as all the school's
> wrestlers, was to be disciplined.
> ("Captain," not "wrestlers," is the subject.)

2. In cases of a compound subject joined by "or" or "nor," the verb is singular if both subjects are singular and plural if both are plural. If one subject is singular and the other plural, the verb must agree in number with the subject nearest to it. A similar rule applies if the sentence includes the correlatives "not only . . . but also."

> Neither the woman nor her sister has
> been found.

> Neither the documents nor the
> pictures have been found.

> Neither the woman nor her sisters
> have been found.

> Not only the players but also the
> coach has been disciplined for
> abusive conduct.

3. A word in apposition does not change the number of the verb.

> Their team, the Flyers, is scheduled
> to play tomorrow.

4. In a relative clause the verb agrees with the antecedent of the relative pronoun, which is the nearest noun or pronoun.

He is one of the students who are
protesting against the university's
investment policies.
("Students" is plural, therefore the
plural verb is the correct choice.)

5. Try not to begin a sentence with words like "it is," "there is," or "here is" because usually they just waste words and make a sentence less powerful. But if you do use them, make sure you do not lose sight of the real subject in determining what verb to use.

There are higher unemployment rates
throughout the Midwest.
(The real subject, "rates," follows the verb.)

6. When they are used as subjects, pronouns like "anyone," "each," "either," "anybody," "everyone," "everybody," "neither," "no one," "nobody," and "someone" take singular verbs.

Each of the women has submitted her
recipe.

Everyone is planning to attend.

7. When "either," "neither," "each," or "every" is used as an adjective, the noun modified takes a singular verb.

Neither course seems to be
a perfect solution.

8. Figuring out the correct verb for use with words such as "any," "none," "some," "all," and "most" is more complex. You have to look at the context. If those words are referring to a unit or a general quantity, they take singular verbs. But if they are referring to individuals, they must be used with plural verbs.

All of the cake was eaten.
(the whole cake as a unit)

All of the soldiers were ordered back.
(all of the individual soldiers)

None of the classes was filled.
(no single one)

None of the administrators agree on the
rules.
(no two individuals)

9. When "number" is preceded by "the," it always takes a singular verb, even if the number of the noun in the prepositional phrase is plural. The reason for the singular verb is that "the number" refers to a unit.

> The number of unemployed people has
> risen in the last month.

However, "a number" refers to an undefined amount but more than one and therefore takes a plural verb.

> A number of unemployed people have
> given up looking for jobs.

10. "Percent" takes a singular verb if it stands alone or is followed by "of" and a singular word. But it takes a plural verb when followed by "of" and a plural word.

> The teacher announced 60 percent is
> a failing grade.

> The teacher said 60 percent of the
> class is failing.

> The teacher said 60 percent of the
> students are failing.

11. Words like "half," "part," "plenty," and "rest" as well as fractions also take either a singular or plural verb, depending on the number in the object of the preposition that follows those words.

> Part of the farms owned by the
> company are up for sale.

> Part of the farmland owned by the
> company is up for sale.

> One-fourth of the students are home
> sick.

> One-fourth of the student body is home
> sick.

12. Elements in a compound subject referring to the same thing or person take a singular verb.

> The chairman and president of the
> board is Edwin Johnson.

13. Subjects that represent units of time, money, measurement, and food take singular verbs.

Five dollars is the standard price
being charged.

Fifty feet is the required width.

Ham and eggs is the special today.

14. Sometimes other words plural in form and collective nouns may take a singular verb. The choice of verb depends on the context. If the reference is to people or things as a unit, use a singular verb. If they are individuals acting separately, use a plural verb.

College athletics has been the
target of much recent criticism.

The school board holds its meetings
the first Monday of the month.

The jury were called at their homes
by reporters after the case ended.

The pair were arrested and charged
with robbery.

The data have been thoroughly
analyzed.
(individual items)

The data is effective.
(a unit)

15. Sometimes a sentence may be grammatically correct but sound awkward when it is following one of the number-agreement rules described in this chapter. If so, rewrite it to avoid that awkwardness.

ORIGINAL: Neither the soldiers who
shot the civilians nor their
commanding officer was convicted.

REVISED: Neither the officer nor
the soldiers under his command who
shot the civilian were convicted.

Correct Pronouns

1. In addition to making sure that verbs agree with their subjects, you must also check to ensure that pronouns agree in number with their antecedent.

Neither of the twins will have to
pay for her own college tuition.
("Neither" is singular, therefore
the pronoun "her" is the
appropriate choice.)

The council has changed the date of
its meeting.
(The reference is to the "council"
as a unit and therefore the pronoun,
as well as the verb, must be
singular.)

2. Names of entities such as companies, organizations, and departments are
singular and therefore the pronouns referring to them should be singular.

General Motors Corp. is expected to
announce its third-quarter earnings
today.

The Bellweather Department Store
will hold its anniversary sale next
week.

3. Pronouns also must be used in the right case.

The candidate who the committee
decided had misused funds withdrew
from the race.
(Because "who" is the subject of the
clause, it is the correct word.)

To whom were the documents sent?
("Whom" is the object of the
preposition "to.")

Information will be sent to whoever
requests it.
("Whoever" is the subject of the
clause.)

That candidate has more
qualifications than he.
("He" is correct because it is the
subject of the implied clause, "than
he does.")

4. Use of possessive pronouns also sometimes causes problems. When using a personal pronoun before a gerund, make it possessive to modify the gerund, which is a noun.

> The judge questioned his handling of
> the case.

5. Remember that "its," "whose," "your," and "their" are possessive pronouns. Do not confuse them with contractions, "it's," "who's," "you're," and "they're."

> The river flooded its banks.
> (possessive)
>
> It's the largest voter turnout in history.
> (contraction)
>
> It doesn't matter whose work is
> finished first.
> (possessive)
>
> Who's favored to win?
> (contraction)

Here is a good check to see if you have selected the right word. If it makes sense to substitute "is" for the apostrophe in "it's" and "who's" and "are" for the apostrophe in "you're" and "they're," you were right in using the contraction. For instance, in checking on the example just given, it makes sense to say: It is the largest voter turnout in history. Therefore, the choice of "it's" is correct. It does not make sense to say: The river flooded it is bank. Therefore, the choice of the possessive pronoun without the apostrophe is correct. However, note that indefinite pronouns like "anyone," "everybody," and "another" do require an apostrophe in forming the possessive.

Possessives of Nouns

Forming possessives of nouns can also be tricky. Remember to start with the basic noun first, using the plural or singular form—whichever is appropriate.

Here are rules to apply in forming possessives.

1. Add " 's" for singular common nouns that do not end in "s."

> boy's, university's, president's

2. Usually add " 's" for singular common nouns that end in "s."

> boss's, bass's

3. However, if a singular common noun ends in "s" and the next word begins with "s," just add an apostrophe to prevent the whole thing from sounding too "sssy."

> the boss' secretary, the bass' solo

4. For a singular proper noun ending in "s," add an apostrophe only, no matter what word follows.

> Socrates', James', Los Angeles'

5. For plural nouns that do not end in "s," add " 's."

> children's, deer's, media's

6. For plural nouns ending in "s," add an apostrophe.

> girls', officers', drivers', the Smiths'

7. Also add only an apostrophe for nouns plural in form even if they are singular in meaning.

> mathematics', measles', United States'

8. If two words are used in a compound relationship indicating they share the object possessed, use the appropriate possessive form only for the word closest to the object possessed.

> John and Sarah's children
>
> her great-grandchild and
> grandchildren's legacy

9. However, if the possession of the object is not joint, use the appropriate possessive form for each word referring to the possessor.

> Canada's and Mexico's future
>
> George's and Henry's tax returns

10. In forming the possessive of compound words, add an apostrophe or " 's," whichever is appropriate, to the word closest to the object possessed.

> the lieutenant colonel's troops
>
> the attorneys general's guidelines
>
> John Jacobson Sr.'s will
>
> the two lieutenant colonels' orders

11. When using the formal names of organizations and institutions, decide how to handle the apostrophe based on how that entity refers to itself.

> Ladies' Home Journal
>
> Veterans Administration
>
> Writer's Market

12. Avoid using the possessive form for inanimate objects.

> ORIGINAL: the chair's leg
>
> REVISED: the chair leg, the leg of the chair

Punctuation

Punctuation can cause endless problems. It was designed to help make written matter easier to follow, but complying with the many rules that have been set down can be a real challenge to the writer.

Here are some of the more common causes of dismay. You can find additional help in the front of some dictionaries.

Commas

One of my students who was struggling to master the rules for commas explained that her high school instructor had told her to insert a comma wherever you would like the reader to pause for a breath. Her readers would have ended up hyperventilating because commas were sprinkled to excess throughout her work.

The decision as to where to insert a comma has to be much more discriminating than that. They should be added only when there is a good prescribed reason to do so.

Here are some problem areas to watch out for.

1. Commas should be used to separate a series of adjectives equal in rank. There is a good way to determine if the adjectives are indeed equal. If you could replace the comma with "and" without changing the sense, the adjectives are equal.

>a careful, meticulous plan
>(It makes sense to say "a careful
>and meticulous plan" because the
>adjectives are equal.)

>a gray fur coat
>(It does not make sense to say "a
>gray and fur coat" because "gray"
>and "fur" are not equal.)

2. Commas are sometimes used to set off clauses. Commas separate two independent clauses connected by a coordinating conjunction such as "and" or "but" when clauses contain little internal punctuation. (If there is such internal punctuation, use a semicolon between the clauses.) Generally, journalists do not use any punctuation before a conjunction like "because" which connects the noun clause with a subordinate or dependent clause. However, be aware experts disagree about dependent clauses introduced by "because." Some say such clauses should always be preceded by a comma.

>Sophomores will register Monday
>through Wednesday, and juniors will
>register the rest of the week.

>The police picked up a man in
>connection with the robbery, but the
>district attorney decided not to
>charge him.

>The building will not be erected
>because funding was not approved.

3. Commas should be used to set off introductory clauses and participial phrases at the beginning of the sentence unless they are very short.

>When the storm had abated shortly
>after midnight, they sailed back to
>the mainland.

>Having checked on the death with the
>coroner, she finished the story and
>called her editor.

4. Commas should be added to set off non-essential (also known as non-restrictive) clauses and phrases from the rest of the sentence. Both essential and non-essential words provide additional information, but the essential clause or phrase cannot be eliminated without altering the basic understanding of the

sentence. If a clause or phrase is essential, commas should not be used, thus encouraging the reader not to skip lightly past those vital words.

> Stringers who are paid by the length
> of their copy may be more likely to
> overwrite.
> (The clause, "who are paid by the
> length of their copy," is essential
> to the meaning of the sentence. It
> is not saying that all stringers
> overwrite, only those paid by the
> length.)

> Scheduled is the 1976 Academy Award-
> winning movie, *One Flew Over the
> Cuckoo's Nest.*
> (Only one movie could be referred to
> here.)

5. Commas are used to set off parenthetical words that are not essential to the meaning of a sentence.

> Meanwhile, police searched the house
> of the suspect.

> However, no pay plan is expected to
> be adopted before December.

6. Commas are used to set off the year in a date that includes the day of the month. But they are not used when just the month and year are written.

> She was born on Dec. 12, 1943, in
> Dallas, Texas.

> The school opened in March 1982.

7. Commas are added before and after the state or country when it appears after the name of a city.

> The wine was bottled in Lyons,
> France, and purchased in the United
> States.

8. Ages used after individuals' names are surrounded by commas.

> John Henderson, 23, will receive the
> award.

9. Use a comma only before a quotation that is a full sentence and not before a partial quotation.

> He said, "I'll return with
> reinforcements who will delay the
> bill's passage."

> He said that he will bring in
> "reinforcements who will delay the
> bill's passage."

Periods

1. The decision whether to use a period with abbreviations often is determined by a newspaper's style. However, generally acronyms (that is, abbreviations that are pronounceable words) do not require periods unless they are unrelated words.

> UNESCO (as an abbreviation for
> United Nations Educational,
> Scientific and Cultural
> Organization)

> U.S. (as an abbreviation for United
> States)

2. The period that normally comes at the end of a sentence is not added to the period after an abbreviation at the end of the sentence.

> He will arrive at 9 p.m.

3. Do not use a period to mark the end of a quoted sentence that is part of a larger sentence that continues beyond the quote. Instead, use a comma, exclamation point, or quotation mark, whichever is appropriate.

> "We shall continue to fight," she
> promised.

> "When will they return?" he asked.

Semicolons

The semicolon is used only infrequently in news writing.

1. Your main use for a semicolon will probably be to set off parts of a series that contain commas.

> She is survived by her daughters,
> Linda and Carol Smith, both at home;
> her sister, Jane Barlin of
> Lancaster, Pa.; and her brother,
> Henry Tompkins of Athens, Ga.

2. Although the semicolon may technically be used to separate two independent clauses, it is usually preferable to use a conjunction or to separate the clauses into two sentences, unless you are after a special literary effect, as in the following example.

> For the contributor it meant a small
> donation; for the starving children
> it means another week of life.

Quotation Marks

1. With quotations that continue beyond a single paragraph, put open quotation marks at the beginning of the quotation and of each paragraph in which the quote continues. But place the ending quotation marks only at the culmination of the quoted matter. Make an exception, however, if the quoted matter at the end of the paragraph is not a full sentence. In that case, put close-quote marks at the end of the partial quotation.

> He said his opponent has been
> "cheating and deceiving the
> voters."
> "I will work hard to end his reign
> as governor," he said.

2. When writing for the many newspapers that follow *The Associated Press Stylebook*, use quotation marks with titles of movies; plays; operas; songs; poems; television programs; lectures; speeches; works of art; and books, except the Bible and reference books. Do not use quotation marks with newspaper and magazine titles.

3. The period and comma always go inside quotation marks, but the question mark, semicolon, and exclamation point are put inside the quote marks only if they are part of the quoted material.

> The principal announced, "The
> school lockers will be searched by
> police officers."

"The river will be cleaned up within
2 years," he promised.

"When will the funds be allocated?"
she asked.

Who directed "On Golden Pond"?

Colons

1. The colon is used to hail with a flourish that which follows. You might want to use it to announce lists, quotations, or complete sentences.

2. The capitalization of the word after the colon varies, depending on the circumstances. If what follows is a complete sentence, capitalize the initial letter. If it is a list or anything else that is not in sentence form, do not capitalize.

He made only this brief statement to
the press: "My fate is in the hands
of the jury."

On the agenda are the following
items: election of a new president,
approval of a budget change, and an
amendment of the zoning regulation.

3. If you are introducing a short list and do not use "the following" or "as follows" in that introduction, you do not need a colon.

Agenda items include election of a
new president, approval of a budget
change, and an amendment of the
zoning regulation.

Dashes

1. When the words following the introduction are brief or a more abrupt break is required, use a dash instead of a colon, especially if you're writing a piece, like a feature, with a more informal tone. A dash can give you the same kind of emphasis and change of pace that a pause can give a stand-up comic. Use it creatively. It can be especially effective in ending a sentence with a surprising or ironic twist.

> He kissed his wife good-bye, took
> his children to school, and went off
> to his office—where he wrote a
> farewell note and fatally shot
> himself.

2. Dashes can be useful in listings where you want to suggest varying actions taken by the subject referred to in the main part of the sentence and not keep repeating the subject.

> The board also voted to:
> —hire an additional physical education teacher.
> —seek bids for a new roof for the high school.
> —give the superintendent of schools
> an additional $2,000 per year.

If you use this kind of list, make sure that the words following the dash are parallel in structure and work to complete the introductory part of the sentence. In the example just given, all are verbs that logically follow the introductory section, "The board also voted to:."

3. Most typewriters do not have dash keys. Use two hyphens to indicate a dash.

Hyphens

1. Unless the style of the newspaper for which you are writing specifically dictates otherwise, use a hyphen when a compound modifier precedes a noun. However, do not use a hyphen to link the adverb "very" or any adverb that ends in "ly."

> He described the 41-year-old student
> as ready to handle the very
> demanding part-time job for which
> she was applying.

2. Because rules on whether to use hyphens after prefixes such as "pre," "ex," and "anti" and before suffixes such as "in" and "wide" may vary, check with the rules being followed by the paper for which you are writing.

Assorted Reminders

And here are a hodgepodge of other reminders of rules often broken.

1. Avoid sentence fragments, unless they are deliberately created for special effect. Sentence fragments are incomplete sentences that lack a subject, a predicate, and/or a complete thought.

> Fingerprints were discovered at the
> scene of the crime. Those of the
> suspect, John Jenkins, who has been
> charged with robbery.
> (The words after the first period
> are an example of a fragment and
> should not stand alone.)

But as in the example that follows, fragments work well if they serve a special purpose.

> Which candidate did the voters pick
> to lead their state? The man who
> has been charged with fraud and
> embezzling.

Or how about this excerpt from a review of the play "The Force of Habit" by Tom Kunkel writing in *The Miami Herald?*

> No sir, it's not like when I was a kid. Or when my dad was a kid. Or when
> my dad's dad was a kid. Back then, nuns were nuns, we're all inclined to agree
> over an occasional beer, and if you did not do your homework you damn well
> might have one popping a pencil up and down on your head. Or lacing your
> knuckles with a wooden pointer. Or at the very least putting you in mortal
> fear for your soul. It was, after all, just another aspect of that mysterious life
> passage known as the Catholic education, not something anyone who went
> through it's apt to shake.

Kunkel's review rolls along with one fragment after another. But it works. The sentence fragments in the hands of a skillful writer help create the kind of stream-of-consciousness sort of feeling so appropriate for his remembrance of days gone by when he was a kid.

    2. On the other hand, run-on sentences, that is, those that do not quit when they should, are also a problem. The problem sometimes occurs when writers link together two independent clauses with commas but no conjunction. The solution usually is to change the comma to a period or semicolon or add an appropriate conjunction.

> ORIGINAL: Thompson won the primary,
> Henderson won the general election.

> REVISED: Thompson won the primary,
> but Henderson won the general
> election.

Like sentence fragments, run-on sentences may also occasionally be used to create special effects. They can quicken the pace with a rush of words or slacken it with a slow, meandering kind of feeling.

3. Be careful to subordinate the minor ideas, not the main thrust of the sentence. Make sure, for instance, that you have not placed the main idea in a clause starting with "which" or "when," or in a participial or infinitive phrase.

> ORIGINAL: Having been struck by an overhead beam at the construction site, he was taken to the hospital.

> REVISED: He was struck by an overhead beam at the construction site and taken to the hospital.

4. Misplaced modifiers, especially adverbs, often create problems. Words such as "hardly," "nearly," "only," and "almost" should be as close as possible to the words they modify. Placing the modifiers incorrectly can change the meaning of the sentence. Notice how the meaning of the sentences in the examples below changes with the placement of the modifier, "only."

> Only pollsters predict that Frank Nelson will win the primary.

> Pollsters only predict that Frank Nelson will win the primary.

> Pollsters predict that only Frank Nelson will win the primary.

> Pollsters predict that Frank Nelson only will win the primary.

> Pollsters predict that Frank Nelson will win the only primary.

> Pollsters predict that Frank Nelson will win the primary only.

5. Watch out for dangling modifiers, which most frequently are at the beginning of sentences and often are participial or infinitive phrases. Here is an example of a dangling participial phrase.

> ORIGINAL: Having financed the car through the bank, it will take 3 years to pay for it.

REVISED: Having financed the car
through the bank, he expects to pay
for it in 3 years.
(In this revised version, "having
financed" is appropriately
positioned to modify "he.")

6. Through comparing one thing with another, you can often give impact to the description, but be careful not to mix your metaphors, as in this example.

The young senator fired the first
volley in the storm of controversy,
then brought in reinforcements.

(Storm clouds over the battlefield
only serve to confuse the metaphor.
Leave them out.)

APME Suggestions

The Associated Press Managing Editors Writing-Editing Committee (APME) compiled a list of 50 errors commonly encountered in newspaper writing. Most involve problems with correct word usage, and some point out spelling and grammar errors. Here is the list as compiled by those editors.

1. **Affect, effect**. Generally, affect is the verb; effect is the noun. "The letter did not affect the outcome." "The letter had a significant effect." BUT effect is also a verb meaning to bring about: Thus: "It's almost impossible to effect change."

2. **Afterward, afterwards**. Use afterward. The dictionary allows use of afterwards only as a second form.

3. **All right**. That's the way to spell it. The dictionary may list alright as a legitimate word but it's not acceptable in standard usage, says Random House.

4. **Allude, elude**. You allude to (or mention) a book. You elude (or escape) a pursuer.

5. **Annual**. Don't use first with it. If it's the first time, it can't be annual.

6. **Averse, adverse**: If you don't like something, you're averse (or opposed) to it. Adverse is an adjective: Adverse (bad) weather, adverse conditions.

7. **Block, bloc**: A bloc is a coalition of persons or a group with the same

purpose or goal. Don't call it a block, which has some 40 dictionary definitions.

8. **Compose, comprise**. Remember that you compose things by putting them together. Once the parts are put together, the object comprises or includes or embraces the parts.

9. **Couple of**. You need the of. It's never "a couple tomatoes."

10. **Demolish, destroy**. They mean to do away with completely. You can't partially demolish or destroy something, nor is there any need to say totally destroyed.

11. **Different from**. Things and people are different from each other. Don't write that they're different than each other.

12. **Drown**. Don't say someone was drowned unless an assailant held the victim's head under water. Just say the victim drowned.

13. **Due to, owing to, because of**. We prefer the last.

> WRONG: The game was canceled due to rain.

> STILTED: Owing to the rain, the game was canceled.

> RIGHT: The game was canceled because of rain.

14. **Ecology, environment**. They're not synonymous. Ecology is the study of the relationship between organisms and their environment.

> RIGHT: The laboratory is studying the ecology of man and the desert.

> RIGHT: There is much interest in animal ecology these days.

> WRONG: Even so simple an undertaking as maintaining a lawn affects ecology.

> RIGHT: Even so simple an undertaking as maintaining a lawn affects our environment.

15. **Either:** It means one or the other, not both.

> WRONG: There were lions on either side of the door.

RIGHT: There were lions on each
side of the door.

16. **Fliers, flyers**: Airmen are fliers. Handbills are flyers. (The latest AP stylebook now suggests that "fliers" be used for handbills also.)

17. **Flout, Flaunt.** They aren't the same words; they mean completely different things and they're very commonly confused. Flout means to mock, to scoff or to show disdain for. Flaunt means to display ostentatiously.

18. **Funeral service.** A redundant expression. A funeral is a service.

19. **Head up**. People don't head up committees. They head them.

20. **Hopefully**. One of the most commonly misused words, in spite of what the dictionary may say. Hopefully should describe the way the subject feels. For instance:

Hopefully, I shall present the plan
to the president.
(This means I will be hopeful when I
do it.)

But it is something else again when you attribute hope to a non-person. You may write:

Hopefully, the war will end soon.
(This means you hope the war will
end soon, but it is not what you are
writing. What you mean is: I hope
the war will end soon.)

21. **Imply and infer**. The speaker implies. The hearer infers.

22. **In advance of, prior to.** Use before; it sounds more natural.

23. **It's, its.** Its is the possessive, it's is the contraction of it is.

24. **Lay, lie.** Lay is the action word; lie is the state of being.

WRONG: The body will lay in state
until Wednesday.

RIGHT: The body will lie in state
until Wednesday.

RIGHT: The prosecutor tried to lay
the blame on him.

However, the past tense of lie is lay.

RIGHT: The body lay in state from
Tuesday until Wednesday.

WRONG: The body laid in state from
Tuesday until Wednesday.

The past participle and the plain past tense of lay is laid.

RIGHT: He laid the pencil on the
pad.

RIGHT: He had laid the pencil on
the pad.

RIGHT: The hen laid an egg.

25. **Leave, let.** Leave alone means to depart from or cause to be in solitude. Let alone means to be undisturbed.

WRONG: The man had pulled a gun on
her but Mr. Jones intervened and
talked him into leaving her alone.

RIGHT: The man had pulled a gun on
her but Mr. Jones intervened and
talked him into letting her alone.

RIGHT: When I entered the room I
saw that Jim and Mary were sleeping
so I decided to leave them alone.

26. **Less, fewer.** If you can separate items in the quantities being compared, use fewer. If not, use less.

WRONG: The Rams are inferior to the
Vikings because they have less good
linemen.

RIGHT: The Rams are inferior to the
Vikings because they have fewer good
linemen.

RIGHT: The Rams are inferior to the
Vikings because they have less
experience.

27. **Like, as.** Don't use like for as or as if. In general, use like to compare with nouns and pronouns; use as when comparing with phrases and clauses that contain a verb.

WRONG: Jim blocks the linebacker
like he should.

RIGHT: Jim blocks the linebacker
as he should.

RIGHT: Jim blocks like a pro.

28. **Marshall, marshal.** Generally, the first form is correct only when the word is a proper noun: John Marshall. The second form is a verb form: Marilyn will marshal her forces. And the second form is the one to use for a title: Fire Marshal Stan Anderson, Field Marshal Erwin Rommel.

29. **Mean, average, median**: Use mean as synonymous with average. Each word refers to the sum of all components divided by the number of components. Median is the number that has as many components above it as below it.

30. **Nouns.** There's a growing trend toward using them as verbs. Resist it. Host, headquarters and author, for instance, are nouns, even though the dictionary may acknowledge they can be used as verbs. If you do, you'll come up with a monstrosity like: "Headquartered at his country home, John Doe hosted a party to celebrate the book he had authored."

31. **Oral, verbal:** Use oral when use of the mouth is central to the thought; the word emphasizes the idea of human utterance. Verbal may apply to spoken or written words; it connotes the process of reducing ideas to writing. Usually, it's a verbal contract, not an oral one, if it's in writing.

32. **Over and more than.** They aren't interchangeable. Over refers to spatial relationships: the plane flew over the city. More than is used with figures: In the crowd were more than 1,000 fans.

33. **Parallel construction.** Thoughts in series in the same sentence require parallel construction.

WRONG: The union delivered demands
for an increase of 10 percent in
wages and to cut the work week to 30 hours.

RIGHT: The union delivered demands
for an increase of 10 percent in
wages and for a reduction in the
work week to 30 hours.

34. **Peddle, pedal.** When selling something, you peddle it. When riding a bicycle or similar form of locomotion, you pedal it.

35. **Pretext, pretense:** They're different, but it's a tough distinction. A pretext is that which is put forward to conceal a truth.

He was discharged for tardiness, but
this was only a pretext for general
incompetence.

A pretense is a "false show"; a more overt act intended to conceal personal feelings.

My profuse compliments were all
pretense.

36. **Principle, principal.** A guiding rule or basic truth is a principle. The first, dominant, or leading thing is principal. Principle is a noun; principal may be a noun or an adjective.

37. **Redundancies to avoid:**

Easter Sunday.   Make it Easter.

Incumbent Congressman.   Congressman.

Owns his own home.   Owns his home.

The company will close down.   The company will close.

Jones, Smith, Johnson and Reid were all convicted.   Jones, Smith, Johnson and Reid were convicted.

Jewish rabbi.   Just Rabbi.

8 p.m. tonight.   All you need is 8 tonight or 8 p.m. today.

During the winter months.   During the winter.

Both Reid and Jones were denied pardons.   Reid and Jones were denied pardons.

I am currently tired.   I am tired.

Autopsy to determine the cause of death.   Autopsy.

38. **Refute.** The word connotes success in argument and almost always implies an editorial judgment.

WRONG: Father Bury refuted the
arguments of the pro-abortion
faction.

RIGHT: Father Bury responded to
the
arguments of the pro-abortion
faction.

39. **Reluctant, reticent.** If he doesn't want to act, he is reluctant. If he doesn't want to speak, he is reticent.

40. Say, said. The most serviceable words in the journalist's language are the forms of the verb to say. Let a person say something, rather than declare or admit or point out. And never let him grin, smile, frown or giggle something.

41. Slang. Don't try to use "with-it" slang. Usually a term is on the way out by the time we get it in print.

42. Spelling. It's basic. If reporters can't spell and copy editors can't spell, we're in trouble. Some ripe ones for the top of your list:

> It's consensus, not concensus.
>
> It's restaurateur, not restauranteur.
>
> It's dietitian, not dietician.

43. Temperatures. They may get higher or lower, but they don't get warmer or cooler.

> WRONG: Temperatures are expected
> to warm up in the area Friday.
>
> RIGHT: Temperatures are expected to
> rise in the area Friday.

44. That, which. That tends to restrict the reader's thought and direct it the way you want it to go; which is non-restrictive, introducing a bit of subsidiary information. For instance:

> The lawnmower that is in the garage
> needs sharpening.
> (Meaning: We have more than one
> lawnmower. The one in the garage
> needs sharpening.)
>
> The lawnmower, which is in the
> garage, needs sharpening.
> (Meaning: Our lawnmower needs
> sharpening. It's in the garage.)
>
> The statue that graces our entry
> hall is on loan from the museum.
> (Meaning: Of all the statues around
> here, the one in the entry hall is
> on loan.)
>
> The statue, which graces our entry
> hall, is on loan.
> (Meaning: Our statue is on loan.
> It happens to be in the entry hall.)

Note that which clauses take commas, signaling they are not essential to the meaning of the sentence.

45. **Under way, not underway**. But don't say something got under way. Say it started or began.

46. **Unique.** Something that is unique is the only one of its kind. It can't be very unique or quite unique or somewhat unique or rather unique. Don't use it unless you really mean unique.

47. **Up.** Don't use it as a verb.

> WRONG: The manager said he would up the price next week.

> RIGHT: The manager said he would raise the price next week.

48. **Who, whom.** A tough one, but generally you're safe to use whom to refer to someone who has been the object of an action. Who is the word when the somebody has been the actor:

> A 19-year-old woman, to whom the room was rented, left the window open.

> A 19-year-old woman, who rented the room, let the window open.

49. **Who's, whose.** Though it incorporates an apostrophe, who's is not a possessive. It's a contraction for who is. Whose is the possessive.

> WRONG: I don't know who's coat it is.

> RIGHT: I don't know whose coat it is.

> RIGHT: Find out who's there.

50. **Would.** Be careful about using would when constructing a conditional past tense.

> WRONG: If Soderholm would not have had an injured foot, Thompson wouldn't have been in the lineup.

> RIGHT: If Soderholm had not had an injured foot, Thompson wouldn't have been in the lineup.

As part of a review of Associated Press stories by the Wisconsin AP Wirewatch Committee, journalism professor Gene Hintz suggested an updating of the list, citing errors that in recent years he has observed to be especially common. Among the additional transgressions set forth by Hintz, who teaches journalism at the University of Wisconsin Oshkosh, were the following:

A, an. Use the article a when it precedes the sound of a consonant. Use the article an when it precedes the sound of a vowel.

> WRONG: It was an historic occasion.

> RIGHT: It was a historic occasion.
> (H is a consonant and pronounced as such.)

> RIGHT: It was an honor. (H is a consonant, but is silent and the O vowel sound takes over.)

> RIGHT: It was an NFL record. (Pronounced en-eff-ell.)

> RIGHT: It was a one-point win. (one is pronounced as if it starts with a consonant.)

After, following. Following is usually a noun, verb or adjective. After is the preferred preposition.

> WRONG: He spoke following dinner.

> RIGHT: He spoke after dinner.

> RIGHT: He had a large following.

> RIGHT: He was following the suspect.

Alleged, allegedly, reportedly. Use with care. Specify who is doing the alleging or reporting. Avoid redundant use and beware of word placement.

> WRONG: The district attorney accused him of allegedly committing murder.

> RIGHT: The district attorney alleged that he committed the crime.

> RIGHT: The district attorney accused him of committing the crime.

> WRONG: He committed the alleged
> crime. (Was it or wasn't it a
> crime?)

> RIGHT: He was accused of committing
> the crime.

Alibi, excuse. An alibi is a plea or fact of having been elsewhere at the commission of an act. An excuse is a justification or explanation for not committing the act.

Apostrophe in numbers. Numbers usually don't own anything. So, apostrophes usually aren't needed except to indicate a dropped number.

> WRONG: It happened in the 1950's.

> RIGHT: It happened in the 1950s.

> RIGHT: It happened in the '50s.

Commas before conjunctions. Commas are not necessary before every conjunction. Writers must differentiate between compound verbs and compound sentences. Commas are used to separate compound sentences, not compound verbs.

> WRONG: The gang problems are small,
> but have the potential to worsen.

> RIGHT: The gang problems are small
> but have the potential to worsen.

Compared with, compared to. Use compared with to illustrate similarities or differences between things. Use compared to only when the intent is to assert that the items are similar.

> WRONG: His average was .331
> compared to .295 a year ago.

> RIGHT: His average was .331
> compared with .295 a year ago.

> RIGHT: He compared his hitting to
> that of Henry Aaron.

Presently, currently, now. Presently means shortly, not at the present time, and should not be confused with currently. While currently or now is sometimes needed for emphasis, in most cases, verb tense makes either word unnecessary.

Proved, proven. Proved is preferred. Proven comes from a term in Scottish law and is archaic.

That, which, who. People and animals with a name take who. Inanimate objects and animals without a name take that and which.

Spelling

Many of the best writers have problems with spelling. I have suspected that otherwise top students I have encountered may be terrible spellers because they read so quickly, they do not take time to look at the individual letters. Or it may be because they are so logical, and English spelling is so illogical. Why is it "defend*a*nt" but "depend*e*nt," "emba*rr*ass" but "ha*r*ass," "*seize*" but "*siege*"? I cannot imagine any logical reason for the discrepancies.

Nor, in many cases, does it help to sound out a word. It is not "flem" but "phlegm," for instance.

Because of the lack of logic, there are no nice, tidy rules that can solve all your spelling problems.

It is no sin to be a lousy speller. But be aware of your shortcomings. Watch out for troublesome words and look them up to make sure you are spelling them correctly.

Be especially on the lookout for this dirty dozen, which Hiley H. Ward (1985) found to be the words most commonly misspelled by new journalists. In writing his journalism textbook, *Professional Newswriting*, he asked about 250 copyeditors to list five words that newcomers to the profession misspell most often. Here are the culprits, in order of frequency of their listing by the editors:

1. Accommodate
2. Occurred
3. Judgment
4. Harass
5. Commitment
6. Embarrass
7. Separate
8. Liaison
9. Cemetery
10. Its, it's
11. Affect, effect
12. Consensus

Sadly, there are no clear-cut rules that will ensure accurate spelling. But here are a few suggestions that may ease your spelling-improvement task a bit.

1. With words ending in "c," add a "k" before an ending beginning with "e," "i," or "y."

> politic, politicking; panic, panicky

2. With verbs ending in "ie," change the "ie" to "y" before adding "ing."

> tie, tying

3. Few verbs end in "efy" and not "ify," and they are not likely to creep into your copy very often. The "efy " words to watch out for are:

> liquefy, putrefy, rarefy, stupefy

4. The formation of the plural of nouns ending in "y" depends on the letter before the "y." If it is preceded by a consonant, form the plural by changing "y" to "i" and adding "es." If it is preceded by a vowel, form the plural by simply adding "s."

> fly, flies; valley, valleys

5. Whether the suffix is correctly spelled "able" or "ible" can usually be determined by the letters to which it is added on. Usually "able" is tacked onto an entire word, whereas "ible" is added to the root of a word that cannot stand alone.

> knowledgeable, commendable;
> irresistible, reprehensible

Watch out: There are exceptions to this rule.

6. One-syllable verbs that end in a consonant (except "h" and "x") double the consonant before the suffixes "ed" and "ing."

> trip, tripped; gel, gelled

7. Most words end in "cede" rather than "sede" or "ceed." Here are the exceptions:

> supersede; proceed, exceed, succeed

These spelling rules leave a lot of words a mystery. Keeping a dictionary within easy reach or using a computer program that catches spelling errors will help avoid problems.

For additional assistance with technical problems, you might want to consult these books that have been written with journalists in mind:

Grammar for Journalists by E. L. Callihan (1979).

Language Skills for Journalists by R. Thomas Berner (1979).

When Words Collide. A Journalists's Guide to Grammar and Style by Lauren Kessler and Duncan McDonald (1984).

Working with Words: A Concise Guide for Media Editors and Writers by Brian S. Brooks and James L. Pinson (1989).

LEGAL AND ETHICAL
CONCERNS

As a journalist, you take on a tremendous responsibility. Sometimes, sitting comfortably in your own home, it can be easy to forget those obligations to the public out there whom you serve.

Once you take on the commitment to provide coverage of an area, you have a responsibility to keep readers of the paper informed about information they need to know.

At the same time, you have a responsibility to report in such a way that you are not unfairly damaging the rights of others.

Court decisions over the years have spelled out what their legal rights are. In this chapter we look at the law as it pertains to journalists to help you understand what your legal responsibilities are and protect yourself from lawsuits (because you personally as the writer of a story as well as the newspaper for which you write can be sued).

You will want to carry out your responsibilities as professionally as possible, often with more rigid standards than those dictated by the law. It is not just a question of whether a certain practice is legally acceptable. Journalists must make sure their practices are fair and careful and up to the highest professional standards possible. That can involve difficult judgment calls. Here we take a look at ethical concerns involved in making such judgments after examining legal issues.

For an understanding of the ever-changing legal standards of today, we must look backward to the earliest history of our country and the thoughts of its founding fathers.

The writers of the Bill of Rights realized the importance of a free press to the smooth functioning of a democratic society. Its protection is a luxury enjoyed by the media of a surprisingly few countries around the world and one that was spelled out in the First Amendment of the First Congress and ratified back in 1791.

That article states: "Congress shall make no law respecting an establishment of religion, or prohibiting the free exercise thereof; or abridging the freedom of speech, or of the press; or the right of the people peaceably to assemble, and to petition the Government for a redress of grievances."

Over the years, courts' interpretations of how that amendment should be applied and weighed against other rights have changed with the times.

Libel

One of the most dramatic changes has taken place in the area of libel law.

Libel is written matter that unjustly damages someone's reputation. It has been defined as matter that exposes an individual to hatred, ridicule, or contempt; that causes others to avoid that person; or that impairs the victim's ability to earn a living. If the court finds an individual's reputation was damaged unfairly, the plaintiff is usually awarded money to compensate for the damage. Provable truth of the information is an effective defense against libel.

Actionable libel generally requires that the material was published, the person was identifiable, and the individual was defamed. A court may determine material was published even if it never was printed in the newspaper. In one of the larger libel settlements in the nation's history, the material involved a memo about accusations that never appeared in the paper.

The case of *Green v. Alton Telegraph Printing Co.* (1982) against the little *Alton* (IL) *Telegraph*, with a circulation of about 38,000, involved a memo checking on allegations against a local building contractor. In the course of checking on accusations that the builder had ties with organized crime, the two reporters working on the story sent a written inquiry to the Justice Department.

The charge was never substantiated and a story about it never published. But the memo to the Justice Department ended up causing the contractor to lose financial backing. The case was settled out of court for $1.4 million. (Originally the plaintiff had won a $9.2 million judgment against the defendant; but the paper filed for bankruptcy protection and a settlement was worked out.)

As for the guideline that actionable libel must involve someone who was identifiable, remember, a name does not necessarily have to have been used.

Other information in the story may enable readers to determine the victim's identity.

Privilege, Fair Comment

Among defenses that might be used in a libel case are what are called *privilege* and *fair comment*.

So-called "absolute privilege" has been extended to government officials to allow them to speak freely. If they are acting in their official capacity, whether or not their statements are true, they cannot be sued for defaming others. In addition, everyone participating in a government proceeding enjoys such a privilege.

Journalists who report those statements made during official government proceedings have been granted what is called *qualified privilege*. If they report such information fully, fairly, and accurately, they are protected from libel suits, even if the information might be false.

As a result, when you cover conflicting statements at a trial, knowing full well that one side is false, you have little to worry about from libel action. Just make sure that you are presenting the total picture of what took place during the proceedings.

Another protection, the right of fair comment, enables journalists to express their opinions about matters of public interest. Thus, writers of opinion pieces can publish unfavorable comments about politicians, restaurants, artists, and movies and the efforts of others who deliberately offer their work to the public for approval.

Public Figure

Additional protection against libel actions was established in 1964 when the U.S. Supreme Court ruled in *The New York Times v. Sullivan* (1964) that to win a suit, a public official must prove a journalist acted with malice, even if the piece contains factual errors.

The case involved an advertisement of a civil-rights group that the *Times* published. The ad stated that police officers with shotguns and tear gas had surrounded an Alabama campus. L. B. Sullivan, who was Montgomery's commissioner for public affairs, complained the ad had several errors. The Supreme Court ruled against Sullivan.

In writing the majority opinion, Justice William Brennan Jr. defined the malice rule. He said a public official can only recover for a defamatory falsehood relating to his official conduct if "he proves that the statement was made with 'actual malice,' that is, with the knowledge that it was false or with a reckless disregard of whether it was false or not."

The Sullivan rule still stands. Up until the mid-1970s, a widening range of individuals was held to be within the category of those who must establish malice. At that point the Supreme Court became less sympathetic to the press in deciding whether or not the plaintiff was a public person.

In 1967, during the period when it was making the media's defense job easier, the U.S. Supreme Court stated the guidelines of *The New York Times* case apply not just to public officials but to public figures. That year in *Curtis Publishing Co. v. Butts* (1967), the court decided that Wallace Butts, the athletic director at the University of Georgia, was a public figure.

In a combined case, that same year the Supreme Court justices also decided in *Associated Press v. Walker* (1967), that Edwin Walker, a former Army general who the Associated Press reported had led a charge to try to prevent black student James Meredith from entering the University of Mississippi, was a public figure.

In the case of *Rosenbloom v. Metromedia, Inc.* (1971), the court expanded the category of public figures to include private individuals involved in matters of general and public interest. The plaintiff had been charged with distributing nudist magazines.

Justice Brennan wrote, "If a matter is a subject of public or general interest, it cannot suddenly become less so merely because a private individual is involved, or because in some sense the individual did not 'voluntarily' choose to become involved."

After the Rosenbloom case, however, the Supreme Court began to make it easier for complainants to sue the media successfully for libel.

In *Gertz v. Robert Welch, Inc.* (1974) the court ruled that Elmer Gertz was not a public figure because he did not have "general fame or notoriety in the community" and did not "thrust himself into the vortex" of the public issue, "nor did he engage the public's attention in an attempt to influence its outcome."

Gertz was an attorney hired to file a civil suit against a Chicago policeman who had fatally shot a youth. *American Opinion*, published by the John Birch Society, implied he had a criminal record, said he had designed a national campaign to discredit the police, and called him a Communist fronter and a Leninist.

The court ruled in the Gertz case that in libel suits brought by private individuals, states were free to require standards of proof less stringent than the actual-malice test as long as those standards involved some degree of fault. The First Amendment, according to the court ruling, would not be infringed upon if a private individual recovered for libel published as a result of negligence though without actual malice. And in many states that category of non-public plaintiffs (enlarged by the Gertz decision) is only required to prove that a journalist was negligent.

In some jurisdictions, private individuals can receive punitive damages only if they establish malice but can recover actual damages for injuries such as impairment of reputation and mental anguish without showing malice.

Indeed, some states use the same standards for private citizens as for public figures. But a greater number of states give private individuals more protection.

The Supreme Court continued to narrow its definition of public figures in the case of *Time, Inc. v. Firestone* (1976). Time had argued that Mary Alice Firestone, a prominent socialite who was involved in a much-publicized divorce, was a public figure. The court disagreed.

And in *Hutchinson v. Proxmire* (1979), the court ruled that a scientist conducting research for the federal government also is not a public figure. Drawing on the Gertz rule, the court said he "did not thrust himself or his views into public controversy to influence others."

The Supreme Court has been rejecting the argument that an individual is a public figure because of the events that led to the story at issue in cases in which they did not seek the limelight by injecting themselves into public debate or by other means.

The definition of a public figure has changed with the makeup of the Supreme Court, and therefore it is hard to know what a future court may rule. It is a vague area. As a Georgia judge, Alexander Lawrence, was quoted as saying, "Defining a 'public figure' is much like trying to nail a jellyfish to the wall."

The guidelines for what has to be proved in a case involving a public figure were spelled out to the jury in a highly publicized libel case, *Sharon v. Time, Inc.* (1985). Editors are hoping that the Federal Judge Abraham Sofaer's method of submitting the case to the jury one step at a time will be adopted in the future by other judges instructing juries.

In the case, conducted in the United States District Court in New York City, former Israeli Defense Minister Ariel Sharon had sued Time Inc. for $50 million over a 1983 story about an Israeli government investigation into the massacre of Palestinian refugees in Beirut.

Judge Sofaer told the jury they had to find: (a) that the article was defamatory; (b) that it was false; and (c) that it was published with reckless disregard for the truth. The plaintiff lost the case because the jury found that he established only that the article was defamatory and false and not that the *Time* reporter and editors had reason to doubt its truthfulness.

Journalists were further aided by a couple of 1986 Supreme Court cases. In *Anderson v. Liberty Lobby* (1986) the Supreme Court ruled that in pretrial proceedings public figures must provide "clear and convincing" evidence of malice if the case is to be allowed to go to trial.

The other Supreme Court case, *Philadelphia Newspapers, Inc. v. Hepps*, (1986) established that in cases involving matters of public concern, plaintiffs have the burden of proving the damaging statements are false. The decision held unconstitutional a Pennsylvania law that required media defendants to prove what they had published was true.

In writing the ruling against Maurice Hepps, owner of a beer-sales operation whom *Philadelphia Inquirer* articles had linked to organized crime, Sandra Day O'Connor no doubt eased some of the fears of those concerned about a possible anti-media outlook on the Reagan administration Supreme Court.

"To insure that free speech of matters of public concern is not deterred," Ms. O'Connor wrote, "we hold that the common law presumption that defamatory speech is false cannot stand when a plaintiff seeks damages against a media defendant for speech of public concern." It remains to be seen how public concerns will be defined.

The decision should help combat harassment suits against the media.

Journalists are also fighting back against harassment by successfully counter-suing against individuals who have filed frivolous libel suits.

Outside help in libel cases has come from both sides. The Libel Prosecution Resource Center opened by the American Legal Foundation helps plaintiffs, and the journalists' friend is the Libel Defense Resource Center.

Protecting Yourself

What can you as a stringer learn from these legal guidelines about libel? Be very careful before writing anything that would tarnish someone's character. That is not to say that you should not report negative things about people. Often that is an important part of your job as a watchdog of the community. But make sure the information is true. Some papers have established guidelines on the extent of proof needed to publish the allegation. For instance, journalists may be required to have written documentation and/or at least two sources who will verify that the accusations are true.

Sometimes, to avoid problems, it is best to write up an incident without identifying the person involved. Take, for instance, this example. A suspect is being held in a murder case and although it is likely charges will be filed against that individual, the person has not yet been charged. Your editor probably will not want you to name the suspect until he or she is charged, yet will want to let readers know that someone has been apprehended in connection with the case. You can avoid problems by reporting that a suspect is being held without identifying that individual. If the person is later let go without being charged, you have not tarnished the reputation of someone police decided they did not have sufficient grounds to hold. If he or she is charged later, you can report the name at that time.

Do not inadvertently stumble into saying something negative without realizing the risk.

At the same time, be aware that you have more latitude when using statements made in a courtroom or during other official proceedings.

Right of Privacy

Another set of legal guidelines important in understanding what you can and cannot do involves the area of privacy rights.

Before the turn of the century there was no legal right to privacy in the United States. More recently courts have begun to recognize the right, and some states have laws to protect it.

The main defenses in privacy actions are newsworthiness and consent.

Even non-public citizens who become unwillingly involved in newsworthy events and matters of public interest lose their right to privacy. The question, then, is when does something become newsworthy. Although that question has often been answered in state courts, few privacy cases have reached the U.S. Supreme Court. Generally, if the person has not consented to have the information published, the courts examine whether the publication of the material was in the public interest, even if it invaded a person's privacy.

However, even when you are reporting on matters of legitimate public interest, you had better think twice about invading someone's private property to get a story. Generally, you must be given permission to go onto the property by the owner or renter, and courts will not look kindly on the use of deception to secure such permission.

But a legal expert has suggested there is a strong First Amendment argument to be made that journalists cannot be convicted of criminal trespass if they follow a news event onto private non-residential land. Jack Landau, former executive director of the Reporters Committee for Freedom of the Press, has argued journalists would seem to have a strong right to cover events such as fires and demonstrations on private property.

Usually you may record and take pictures of what you see and hear in public places (but some states have laws prohibiting the recording of a conversation without the permission of those involved).

Although the laws of libel and privacy are similar, the libel guidelines protect a person's character, whereas the right of privacy protects an individual's peace of mind and sensibilities. Although truth is generally a defense in libel actions, it is not in privacy cases. Therefore, remember you must make sure not only that your stories are truthful but also that they are indeed newsworthy or you have received consent.

However, despite a high level of care, you may still someday find yourself involved in legal action, as many of the reporters for some of the country's greatest papers have. It is a risk that goes with the job. To protect yourself against the cost of such a suit, you may want to consider taking out insurance.

Unfortunately, you are likely to find the price of such individual libel insurance to be prohibitively expensive. Yet the libel insurance policies of some publications may prevent them from assuming responsibility for those not on their regular staff even if they wanted to—leaving you out in the cold.

Because of the dilemma, I have been talking to an insurance company representative about the possibility of a less costly group policy for free lancers, perhaps offered through a journalism organization. I hope that by the time you read this book, some kind of arrangement may have been worked out.

Free Press-Fair Trial

Another legal hurdle can arise when you report on crimes and find yourself amid what has become known as the free press–fair trial controversy.

Media representatives believe they have an obligation to keep the public informed about criminal cases and a right to do so under the free-press provision of the First Amendment. But weighed against that right is the defendant's right to a fair trial guaranteed by the Sixth Amendment to the Constitution.

For the first time the Supreme Court in 1961 overturned the conviction of a criminal in a state court because the justices believed publicity had made it impossible for him to get a fair trial.

In that case, *Irvin v. Dowd,* (1961) the defendant had been charged with six murders. A government prosecutor had issued press releases reporting that he had confessed to all the murders and calling him "Mad Dog Irvin."

In 1966 in *Sheppard v. Maxwell* the court threw out the conviction of Cleveland osteopath Samuel Sheppard, accused of murdering his pregnant wife, stating that extensive and highly inflammatory pretrial publicity had violated his right to a fair trial.

In the wake of that case, members of the legal profession and press met to formulate voluntary guidelines to try to prevent the publication of prejudicial information. In most states there are now guidelines on what information shall be released at the time of an arrest. Usually that information includes the name, address, residence, employment, and marital status of the individual accused; the charge; and the general circumstances surrounding the arrest. Information deemed to be prejudicial is not usually made public. That generally includes confessions and the prior criminal record of the suspect.

Sometimes reporters have encountered judges who have forbidden them to cover judicial proceedings, arguing the need to ensure justice for the defendant. The Supreme Court ruled in *Nebraska Press Association v. Stuart* (1976), a case involving an accused mass murderer, that the court will find orders against reporting open court proceedings unconstitutional unless they are clearly justified.

In 1976 the Supreme Court recognized judges' power to close pretrial hearings when the judge believes the publicity might adversely affect the chance that the defendant would get a fair trial. In that case, *Gannett v. DePasquale* (1979), the court ruled on the action of a judge who had barred the press and public from pretrial hearings involving charges against a 16-year-old accused of the murder of a policeman.

But although the Supreme Court allowed the closing of pretrial hearings in that case, the next year it ruled in *Richmond Newspapers v. Virginia* (1980) that the press as well as the public have the right to attend criminal trials.

Check with your editor about what to do if you are denied access to judicial proceedings.

Revealing Sources

You may someday also find yourself in conflict with the courts over your reluctance to reveal the identity of sources. The Supreme Court ruled in *Branzburg v. Hayes* (1972), that journalists have no right under the First Amendment to refuse to tell grand juries the names of confidential sources and the information they received from those sources.

But in the majority opinion Justice Byron White wrote: "At the Federal level Congress has freedom to determine whether a statutory newsman's privilege is necessary and desirable and to fashion standards and rules as narrow or broad as deemed necessary."

Congress has not acted, probably in part because journalists themselves have mixed feelings about such national legislation. Some journalists fear that if Congress adopts one law to protect journalists, it might someday adopt other regulations that limit journalists' freedom.

But although there is no federal legislation, a number of states have enacted shield laws of varying kinds, enabling reporters to refuse to reveal sources. However, the protection is not absolute, as one of the most celebrated cases in the area demonstrated (*In re Farber*, 1978).

Myron Farber, a reporter for *The New York Times*, and his newspaper were found in contempt of court in New Jersey when they refused to give a judge files in a murder case.

Defendant Mario Jascalevich, a physician, had been charged with multiple murders in a hospital. He was brought to trial after the *Times* published a series of articles by Farber, and the defense demanded the confidential files kept by Farber.

New Jersey had enacted a shield law. The journalist refused to turn over the files, citing the shield law, but Farber was convicted. The Supreme Court declined to review the case, allowing the conviction to stand. Farber spent 40 days in jail, and the *Times* was fined $185,000.

The warning from this case is that shield laws may offer little or no protection against contempt citations for refusing to provide confidential information, especially if the defense can prove the notes are material and relevant in the criminal case and alternative sources of information have been exhausted. Only for the most compelling reasons should you promise confidentiality and get yourself and your paper into this legal conflict—and it is a good idea not to make such a promise before checking with your editor.

In general it is important to work closely with your editor on stories with potential legal problems. Point out what you see as possible danger areas to your editor in upcoming stories and discuss how the articles should be handled.

Many newspapers have their own attorneys or work regularly with a local lawyer on legal questions. Editors will frequently ask a lawyer to read before publication a story that questions someone's character and therefore might generate legal action. Do not be offended if your story is reviewed in this way. It can help a newspaper serve its watchdog role in as hard-hitting a way as possible without encountering legal difficulties.

But often it is not the long-term investigation that everyone is perusing so carefully that touches off a libel suit. Frequently it is a more routine item whose potential danger was easily overlooked. For instance, a war veteran collected $10,000 in an out-of-court settlement after capturing a purse snatcher during a chase. The paper had reversed their names, identifying him as the thief. So be on the lookout for hazardous copy, no matter how routine the story.

If you need further assistance in determining how you stand legally, call the Legal Assistance Hotline run by the Reporters Committee for Freedom of the Press in Washington, DC.[1]

Ethical Concerns

But it is not enough to make sure you have not stepped on anyone's legal rights. As a journalist, you must also be concerned with meeting the ethical standards of a profession with heavy responsibility for helping to ensure the proper workings of a democracy. And in recent years those standards have become ever more stringent.

You may frequently find yourself in the position of writing stories in which others' conduct is criticized. Your own conduct must be beyond reproach.

Sometimes decisions about what is correct and incorrect conduct are clear-cut. Obviously it was wrong for former *Washington Post* reporter Janet Cooke

---

[1]The phone number for the hotline is 1-800-336-4243.

to have created a mythical 8-year-old heroin addict on her way to becoming a Pulitzer Prize winner.

In a vivid and skillful style she wrote a story published in 1980:

> Jimmy is 8 years old and a third-generation heroin addict, a precocious little boy with sandy hair, velvety brown eyes and needle marks freckling the babysmooth skin of his thin brown arms. . . .

> Jimmy's world is a world of hard drugs, fast money and the good life he believes both can bring. Every day, junkies casually buy heroin from Ron, his mother's live-in lover, in the dining room of Jimmy's home. They "cook" it in the kitchen and "fire up" in the bedrooms. And every day, Ron or somebody else fires up Jimmy, plunging a needle into his bony arm, sending the fourth grader into a hypnotic nod.

But there was no Jimmy, no live-in lover making the 8-year-old into an addict. Cooke had been swept up in the ambition to win a place as a top-ranked reporter. But with the exposure of the deception, at one sweep she lost the coveted Pulitzer Prize, her job at the *Post*, and her reputation.

No one would argue it was acceptable behavior for a reporter to create a character and pretend he was real in a story dramatizing the evils of the spread of heroin.

Other issues raised by the incident are a bit more complex. For instance, is it all right for writers to present a composite character made up of characteristics of various individuals when they cannot find an appropriate person with the various characteristics they need to illustrate a particular story? At one point, Cooke told her interrogators Jimmy was such a composite.

Certainly if the character was indeed a composite figure, the story should have said so—and it did not. And many editors would agree that such composites should not be used even with an explanation because they tend to deceive the public and unduly sensationalize the problem.

A further ethical question that arises out of the Cooke case is whether the paper should have intervened to help the youth, if he really existed. Is it ethical for a reporter to know about such a sad case and stand by and allow the problem to continue without notifying authorities? Yes, you are a journalist telling the tale, but you are also a fellow human concerned about the plight of others.

As in this case, judgment calls are often involved in deciding how to handle news stories. And journalists may disagree about the best approach. Sometimes there are no clear-cut answers. But it is important to be aware of the ethical issues and the ramifications involved.

Here are some other issues with which journalists are confronted as they do their jobs.

Anonymous Sources

Is it ever appropriate to use anonymous sources? Yes, but newspaper editors have been less lenient in allowing use of anonymous sources in recent years, especially in light of the Janet Cooke problem.

As a result of the Cooke story, journalists throughout the country pondered how to prevent such deception from slipping past editors, who in the case of Cooke's piece included superjournalist Bob Woodward of Watergate fame.

Cooke understandably had written the story so as not to identify the boy. But no editors at the *Post* had required her to identify him confidentially to them. Today your editors will probably not allow you to get away with such a procedure. You will likely be asked to share the confidential information with them, with the understanding that they will not violate any confidentiality you have promised a source.

You should have a very good reason before you promise anonymity. Will revealing their names place sources in physical danger, cause them to lose their jobs, or have some other dire effect? If so, your editor will probably permit you to run the story without the name. But do not allow yourself to be manipulated by those who want to take potshots at others without identifying themselves. Overuse of anonymous sources contributes to the credibility problem the press is facing with its public.

Even if you are unable to use the name, try to get your source to allow you to identify him or her to the extent possible without causing harm. For instance, although a school teacher giving you information declined to allow you to use her name, you might be able to identify her as a teacher. Readers will place more stock in the comments of someone in a position to know about what is said.

Think very carefully before you agree to keep remarks off the record. Sometimes it is better to decline to listen to such remarks and hope your sources will change their minds and speak on the record. But if you do agree not to use the comments, do not go back on your word.

Many papers have established guidelines for handling anonymous sources. Here is what *The Washington Post*'s stipulates:

> This newspaper is pledged to discuss the source of all information unless disclosure would endanger the source's security. When we agree to protect a source's identity, that identity will not be made known to anyone outside the *Post*.

> Before any information is accepted without full attribution, reporters must make every reasonable effort to get it on the record. If that is not possible, reporters should consider seeking the information elsewhere. If that in turn is not possible, reporters should request an on-the-record reason for protecting the source's identity and should include the reason in the story.

In any case, some kind of identification is almost always possible—by department or position, for example—and should be reported.

Deception

Is it ever appropriate to use deception in getting a story?

The staff at the *Chicago Sun-Times* decided it was in 1978 when they bought a bar, staffed it with employees of their newsroom, and gathered proof of payoff and corruption in the city inspection system.

Some journalists involved in the selection of Pulitzer Prize winners disagreed with the tactics. The paper, which had been nominated for the Pulitzer, did not receive the prize. Ben Bradlee, a member of the Pulitzer Board and executive editor of *The Washington Post*, questioned how newspapers can fight for integrity when they are less than honest in getting a story.

But many journalists believe the total situation should be examined. If the story is of important public interest and there is no other way to secure the information except through deception, use it, they argue.

Otherwise, be scrupulously forthright in the way you secure information. Identify yourself by name and the paper you represent before asking questions. Do not bluff and say that you have information you indeed do not have to try to confirm it or gather more information. And do not create quotes by using anything except the exact words of the source.

Conflict of Interest

In 1985 ex-*Wall Street Journal* reporter R. Foster Winans was found guilty of criminal counts involving accusations that he told stock speculators about information to be run in the paper before it was published. He had been a contributor to the paper's influential "Heard on the Street" column, which provides analyses and predictions about the future of various companies. The column often seems to affect the price of the stock of those companies after it is run. Clearly, Winans' conduct was unethical, and it was determined to be illegal.

But at what point does a journalist run into conflict-of-interest concerns? Should business reporters own stock in any of the companies about which they write? Should business reporters own any stock at all? Should journalists, no matter what area they cover, own stocks?

Most editors would allow reporters to own the stock if they were not involved in covering news of the company.

And what about outside interests that have no financial ramifications? Should a political reporter work on a presidential campaign? What about a lifestyles reporter? Should reporters be members of outside organizations such as the Sierra Club, the John Birch Society, or even the Chamber of Commerce?

As is true with much in journalism, standards change with the times. Just as judges' decisions are affected by and seem to reflect the attitudes of society at the time, so too do guidelines adopted by journalists.

There was a time when newspaper employees were encouraged to join as many organizations as possible. It helped bring in advertising dollars as well as news tips.

But with the protest generation and general questioning of establishment guidelines in the 1960s and 1970s came questioning of the outside involvement of journalists. In the post-Watergate days many young people were entering the journalism profession because they wanted to make a difference. A large number were activists with determined ideas as to what changes they wanted to see.

Some were discouraged from getting involved in activist organizations because it was viewed as a conflict of interest that prevented them from appearing to be objective reporters. During the height of the concern I heard an editor tell a seminar group at the American Press Institute that his paper even had a rule against the spouses of reporters working for political campaigns because of the conflict of interest it presented.

Such a rule today would no doubt be viewed as an unwarranted intrusion. Today's reporters generally are encouraged to participate actively in the community they serve in order to know what is going on and better understand the needs of their public. But most editors would probably frown upon reporters being part of a group involved in controversies they were assigned to cover. Get involved in community organizations but not controversial ones you have the responsibility for covering.

Conflict-of-interest rules are as much designed to ward against the appearance of conflicts as to prevent actual problems of a reporter losing objectivity. Editors realize that many among their staff will bend over backward to be fair, even if it goes against their interest, because they are professionals. But the public may not view the situation in the same way. The paper wants to avoid any situation that the public might view as compromising.

Freebies

This appearance of being compromised is also in part the reason for the rule against journalists accepting so-called freebies.

In days past it was not uncommon for journalists to be showered with gifts, and not all of them small tokens. Theater tickets, meals at restaurant openings, trips, even cars—all were among the bounty bestowed on these generally poorly paid journalists.

But in recent years the profession has become very sensitive to the potential evils accompanying such largesse. Many newspapers forbid their employees to accept gifts.

But freebies used by reporters in the course of doing their jobs present a more complex problem. Should reporters accept free tickets to plays they are reviewing, passes and plane rides to athletic events they are covering, hotel accommodations for travel pieces they are writing? Different papers have responded in varying ways. Larger papers able to cover all of these areas without free assistance may be inclined to turn down the freebies whereas many smaller papers may find themselves in a more difficult financial situation. Failure to accept the free passes might mean they could not regularly cover the event. Editors have to weigh the situation in setting up policy.

Check with your editor to find out the policy of the paper for which you are writing. You may, for instance, be asked to pay for tickets and seek reimbursement from the paper rather than accept free ones from the theater.

Errors

It is unlikely that journalists in the business for a number of years have not included errors in their stories. Sometime during the course of rushing for a deadline you may write an inaccuracy into the story. And fairly often sources may provide inaccurate information.

Let your editor know as soon as you become aware of any inaccuracy in one of your stories that has been published, whether that error is yours or someone else's. Your editor will decide what to do about it. The policy about handling corrections varies from one paper to another. Smaller errors of little consequence may be ignored. In some papers more significant ones are combined into a special corrections section run on a daily basis. Errors of great significance may be the topic of a special story devoted to the correction.

Fairness

Understand the complexity of the stories you are writing and probe all of their various ramifications. Remember that often there are not only two but many sides to an issue. Keep well enough informed and devote enough time to a story that you are able to present it fairly and thoroughly.

Do not go gunning for someone you just do not happen to like. It is all too easy to make someone look foolish. Try to understand the positions taken by everyone you encounter and present them fairly.

Attempt to keep your own biases from affecting a story. It is impossible to come to a story without preconceived notions—only a non-thinking being could do so. No story is really completely without subjective input. Just selecting a story to write and picking a lead with a certain focus is a subjective process. But be open-minded when you approach a story. You may have thought the focus of a story would go in one direction yet after researching it thoroughly, you find it should go in a very different direction.

Do not sensationalize a story and blow it out of all proportion to help make a name for yourself. It is that kind of conduct that has contributed to the credibility problems of the journalism profession as a whole. Your transgressions can undermine the work of your fellow journalists. Your main guiding principle should be a concern for what best serves the public interest.

Public Watchdog

One of your most significant jobs is to serve as a community watchdog.

Remember that it is not generally in a corporation's interest for its representatives to point out it is polluting the environment, nor is it in an employee's interest to point out his boss is skimming off the profits. In some areas, such as the environmental field, there may be effective watchdog organizations pointing out abuses. But in others it may be up to you, members of the press, to be the sole watchdog.

In serving that role, be especially mindful of the voiceless—the poor and uneducated, prisoners, mental health patients—those who may have a harder time getting society to listen to them yet may have genuine grievances.

In his textbook, *News Reporting and Writing*, Melvin Mencher (1984) described his view of the journalists's commitment. He wrote:

> The journalist who is committed to the open society, to democratic values, has a moral structure from which to work. It seems clear that the journalist must be alert to the institutions and their activities that threaten the right of everyone to take part justly, equally and freely in some kind of meaningful community life. (p. 432)

Determinants of Values

How are the values that affect a journalist's standard of ethics determined? As a free-lance journalist working outside of a newsroom you are missing out on what a study has found to be the most common influence on ethical decision— the day-by-day newspaper environment.

Professors G. Cleve Wilhoit, David Weaver, and Richard Gray (1986) interviewed more than 1,000 journalists from a representative cross-section of print and broadcast news journalists. In the study, sponsored by the Gannett Foundation, 88% listed the day-to-day newsroom environment as a factor that significantly influenced their ethical decisions.

Because you are so far removed from the kinds of ethical discussions that regularly take place in the newsroom, try on your own to be especially conscious of the issues being raised in journalism circles. Subscriptions to publications like *Editor & Publisher* and the *Washington Journalism Review* and membership in the Society of Professional Journalists can prove tremendously helpful.

Attitudes toward journalism ethics have been evolving and changing. Nothing is carved in stone.

Unlike doctors and lawyers, journalists do not have codes that they must follow or risk the right to practice their profession. Journalists, to protect their freedom of expression, have sought to avoid the kind of enforcement mechanism that would be needed for such a code to be effective. Instead, they have attempted to patrol their own ranks.

Many individual newspapers have established their own codes. Ask your editor if the paper for which you write has one. Major journalism organizations, including the American Society of Newspaper Editors, the Associated Press Managing Editors, and the Society of Professional Journalists, also have ethical codes.

Here is an example of a professional organization's code. It contains important rules for all journalists to keep in mind.

The Society of Professional Journalists
Code of Ethics

The SOCIETY of Professional Journalists, Sigma Delta Chi believes the duty of journalists is to serve the truth.

We BELIEVE the agencies of mass communication are carriers of public discussion and information, acting on their Constitutional mandate and freedom to learn and report the facts.

We BELIEVE in public enlightenment as the forerunner of justice, and in our Constitutional role to seek the truth as part of the public's right to know the truth.

We BELIEVE those responsibilities carry obligations that require journalists to perform with intelligence, objectivity, accuracy, and fairness.

To these ends, we declare acceptance of the standards of practice here set forth:

I. RESPONSIBILITY:

The public's right to know of events of public importance and interest is the overriding mission of the mass media. The purpose of distributing news and enlightened opinion is to serve the general welfare. Journalists who use their professional status as representatives of the public for selfish or other unworthy motives violate a high trust.

II. FREEDOM OF THE PRESS:

Freedom of the press is to be guarded as an inalienable right of people in a free society. It carries with it the freedom and the responsibility to discuss, question, and challenge actions and utterances of our government and of our public and private institutions. Journalists uphold the right to speak unpopular opinions and the privilege to agree with the majority.

III. ETHICS:

Journalists must be free of obligation to any interest other than the public's right to know the truth.

1. Gifts, favors, free travel, special treatment or privileges can compromise the integrity of journalists and their employers. Nothing of value should be accepted.

2. Secondary employment, political involvement, holding public office, and service in community organizations should be avoided if it compromises the integrity of journalists and their employers. Journalists and their employers should conduct their personal lives in a manner that protects them from conflict of interest, real or apparent. Their responsibilities to the public are paramount. That is the nature of their profession.

3. So-called news communications from private sources should not be published or broadcast without substantiation of their claims to news values.

4. Journalists will seek news that serves the public interest, despite the obstacles. They will make constant efforts to assure that the public's business is conducted in public and that public records are open to public inspection.

5. Journalists acknowledge the newsman's ethic of protecting confidential sources of information.

6. Plagiarism is dishonest and unacceptable.

IV. ACCURACY AND OBJECTIVITY:

Good faith with the public is the foundation of all worthy journalism.

1. Truth is our ultimate goal.

2. Objectivity in reporting the news is another goal that serves as the mark of an experienced professional. It is a standard of performance toward which we strive. We honor those who achieve it.

3. There is no excuse for inaccuracies or lack of thoroughness.

4. Newspaper headlines should be fully warranted by the contents of the articles they accompany. Photographs and telecasts should give an accurate picture of an event and not highlight an incident out of context.

5. Sound practice makes clear distinction between news reports and expressions of opinion. News reports should be free of opinion or bias and represent all sides of an issue.

6. Partisanship in editorial comment that knowingly departs from the truth violates the spirit of American journalism.

7. Journalists recognize their responsibility for offering informed analysis, comment, and editorial opinion on public events and issues. They accept the obligation to present such material by individuals whose competence, experience, and judgment qualify them for it.

8. Special articles or presentations devoted to advocacy or the writer's own conclusions and interpretations should be labeled as such.

V. FAIR PLAY:

Journalists at all times will show respect for the dignity, privacy, rights, and well-being of people encountered in the course of gathering and presenting the news.

1. The news media should not communicate unofficial charges affecting reputation or moral character without giving the accused a chance to reply.

2. The news media must guard against invading a person's right to privacy.

3. The media should not pander to morbid curiosity about details of vice and crime.

4. It is the duty of news media to make prompt and complete correction of their errors.

5. Journalists should be accountable to the public for their reports and the public should be encouraged to voice its grievances against the media. Open dialogue with our readers, viewers, and listeners should be fostered.

VI. PLEDGE:

Adherence to this code is intended to preserve and strengthen the bond of mutual trust and respect between American journalists and the American people.

The Society shall—by programs of education and other means—encourage individual journalists to adhere to these tenets, and shall encourage journalistic publications and broadcasters to recognize their responsibility to frame codes of ethics in concert with their employees to serve as guidelines in furthering these goals.

CODE OF ETHICS (Adopted 1926; revised 1973, 1984, 1987)

SHOULD YOU BUY
A COMPUTER?

Let's face it, writers and other artistic types may not often be the first on their block to rush out and buy the latest in technological gadgetry. How many of you have an electronic scale that tells you your weight or a smart-alecky car that tells you you had better fasten your seat belt? Or even a videocassette recorder or a combination clock radio-telephone?

Perhaps it is because writers, especially free-lance writers, are so poorly paid they can ill afford to rush to join the technological revolution. Or perhaps it is a resistance to equipment that tends to promote precision and speed rather than spontaneity and individuality.

But the time has arrived for you to consider investing in a computer, if you have not already done so.

In fact, you may be among the small proportion of the population who could make significant use of a home computer. Many a computer buff might be envious of your position. Unlike the families whose computers ended up in a closet because they served little more use than a toy, your computer could both save you time and problems with inaccuracies and add to the quality of your research.

Pros and Cons

It is questionable whether you will find a computer more helpful for handling straightforward typing than a regular typewriter. However, because some computers are in the same price range as an electric typewriter and can offer benefits beyond straight typing, they are well worth considering.

170

And some computer users would argue that even for straight typing a regular typewriter is no match for the word-processing capabilities of a computer. The computer will perform useful tricks like centering copy, correcting letters, and returning to the next line automatically (although it should be noted today's electronic typewriters also have these features).

Furthermore, computers will allow you to delete or move around whole blocks of copy with little effort. The initial versions of the previous two typewritten pages of this manuscript ended up in the wastebasket. With a computer I could merely have wiped out the problem paragraphs and started again.

And you can use computers to search for words in your text that you would like to change. Say, for instance, that consistently throughout the story you spelled the town supervisor's name as "Horten." You discovered you were wrong and it should be "Horton." You can ask your computer to search your story for each time you used the name and correct it.

On the other hand, I find it is harder to organize my thoughts on a computer. The screen does not allow me to see as much of the copy as a typewritten page. True, I could use a printer to make a copy of the story typed on the word processor, but that involves an extra step.

And although it is faster to type up an error-free rendition of the piece on a computer, I find it faster when writing something that does not have to look perfect to use a typewriter, then pencil in changes on the typewritten page because the corrections can be made more quickly. And if after trying out changes, I decide I prefer the original version, I can simply erase the changes and return to the original.

You may or may not find straight writing of a first draft more efficient on a computer. Even *Writer's Digest* magazine's columnist on word processing has reservations.

"I don't believe the art of writing is benefited at all from word processors," wrote Ronald John Donovan (1985) in his initial column, the first draft of which was composed with pen and paper. "It's no problem for a writer to produce good writing with any instrument that may be close at hand" (p. 46).

But, he added, "By contrast, the business of writing is dramatically simplified with a word processor. It doesn't matter how you used to produce multiple drafts, query letters, requests for interviews or whatever. A word processor makes such tasks easier" (p. 46).

Perhaps the most significant advantage for a writer in the business of stringing is the possibility of transmitting your copy directly to computer equipment at your newspaper's office.

No doubt you have experienced the annoyance faced so often by stringers of having your copy altered because the person to whom you dictated your story over the phone misheard what you said. The inaccuracy creeps into the story under your byline, and few but you know it was not your mistake. If it happens very often, it can jeopardize your relationship with your sources, who do not think they can trust you to get the facts right.

With a computer transmitting your story by phone to the newspaper, your editor gets it in just the same form you typed it. The middleman is eliminated, and with that person the increased chance for errors.

In addition, the procedure can save you a lot of time—and for the stringer getting paid by the story, time definitely translates into money. Some feature stories may take as long as a half hour to dictate. That is a half hour you can use to start working on other stories. Multiply the dictation time for a story by the total number of stories you call in over the course of a year and you will appreciate how the computer can start paying for itself quickly.

Check on Compatibility

But before you run out and join the technological revolution, be careful. Make sure the computer you have in mind can interact with your newspaper's computer system. Perhaps your editor can help you with the technical information you need to decide what will and will not work. If not, ask to speak to the electronics technician who takes care of the newspaper's equipment.

Inquire if the full-time reporters are using computers out in the field to write their stories. Find out the brand they use to help determine a type of computer that will be able to interact effectively.

Although most of the copy of the full-time reporters is written up in the newspaper office, they too have occasions when they must transmit their stories to the paper because there is insufficient time to return to the office and write them up. The so-called laptop portable computers they use come in handy for this purpose. And they are especially helpful because if they are covering a meeting or other event on deadline, reporters can begin writing up their story while the proceedings continue.

At *The Seattle Times* reporters can even transmit a story from a remote forest. The reporters have portable computers plus cellular phones, both of which are battery powered.

Portable Computers

Because of the many times you may find it handy to use a computer away from your desk in the rush for deadline, consider purchasing a laptop model.

Much design effort in the computer field has been focused on this area in recent years. As a result, the new little computers—some of which are now under 10 pounds—really are portable, unlike their larger forerunners. Those earlier so-called portable models were much heavier and awkward to carry.

Because many of the laptops are so new, their prices may drop in the future, as often happens with new electronic technology after it has been out on the market for a while. By the time this book comes out, you may decide prices and technology have reached the point when it is time to invest in this useful tool.

If you plan to use a computer solely to write newspaper articles and send them by a modem (short for modulator–demodulator, a device used to convey information to and from computers in various locations via telephone lines), a laptop computer may meet your total needs.

The kind of work you plan to do on a computer will also determine whether your unit should have a disk drive, generally used by desk top computers but not by some portables. The disks can store your copy for future use. The drives read the little disks much like the head on a tape recorder reads a cassette.

These disk drives make storage of large amounts of material easier. Indeed you can use your printer to make paper copies of anything you need to preserve even if you do not have a disk drive. However, you lose out on the advantage of later being easily able to edit with a computer the material you have written and preserved.

If you are writing for magazines that often use long articles as well as newspapers, you will find a computer with adequate provisions for storage of information especially helpful. Often you might want to query a number of different magazine editors about your idea for a story. And because each magazine is a little bit different, you will want to alter that query letter to fit the specific market. Using your computer, you can easily make the needed changes without having to retype the whole letter.

If in addition to writing, you are involved in turning out publications like newsletters and annual reports that entail the use of graphics and other design techniques, a laptop computer may not be the route to go. You may want to look into a desktop computer, such as Apple's Macintosh, which allows you to add these sophisticated touches. Apple recently came out with a portable Macintosh, but you may find it prohibitively expensive. At this writing it was selling for about $6,500.

Because of the limitations of laptop computers, some businesses are giving their employees laptop computers to use in the field or at home and standard, non-portable computers for the office. If you can afford it, you too may want to invest in both. Because that is unlikely, you will have to decide whether today's portables will do everything you need and whether their cost is within the range you care to spend.

Lower Priced Options

You may want instead to buy a less expensive non-portable personal computer. For your purposes you do not have to head to a computer store and buy one of the often pricier models they have to offer. The less expensive brands such as

Commodore and Atari offered at your local low-cost general merchandise stores will probably meet your writing needs.

You may be pleasantly surprised at the prices of such computers today because they have dropped drastically to remain competitive. The cost varies considerably depending on where you buy them and whether you buy them during special sales.

As an example of how inexpensively you can set yourself up with computer equipment, consider this listing in a catalogue of a mail-order discount merchant. The company was advertising a Super Commodore 64C computer with disk drive (and a mysterious action game and free gift thrown in) for $249.95.

Significant discounts for computer equipment are available through mail-order houses. You can find out how to connect with them through their ads in computer magazines. You may prefer to use a local computer store even if its prices are higher so you can feel free to draw upon the expertise of its staff. But I and others have done that, only to have the local store go out of business. And you may find a national discounter who offers expert help. Computer Direct in Barrington, Illinois, for instance, provides a phone number for technical assistance for its customers. And it advertises a trial arrangement that allows you to try its computer merchandise for 15 days and send it back if you are not happy with it.

You must not forget in figuring the cost of your equipment to add the price of a printer, which in some cases can be as much or more than the computer. You will need it in order to produce hard (that is, printed) copy.

Some writers, however, are turning to word processors with printers built in. The price, often about $500, is an incentive as is the ease of use. Their disadvantages are they cannot perform many of the tasks of a more complex piece of computer equipment and are bulky to lug around. But they may be fine for your needs.

Printers

If you are in the market for a separate printer, you will find a rapidly growing variety to pick from. Printer manufacturers are continually looking for new and better ways to put ink on paper. Current types of printers are dot-matrix, daisy-wheel, ink-jet, and laser.

At this point you may decide a dot-matrix printer is your best choice. Generally, they are fast and relatively inexpensive, but the printing is of somewhat poorer quality. The letters produced by some dot-matrix printers tend to be boxy-looking with visible dots that make them appear unprofessional and harder to read. However, the quality of dot-matrix printers has been improving dramatically, and some of the new offerings on the market may be fine for your needs.

Laser printers offer the highest quality, but you may not want to make that large an investment. When you are pricing printers, make sure you consider the cost of supplies for the ink-jet and laser printers along with the original purchase price.

You should consider investing in a fairly high-quality printer. Do not just look for the one with the lowest price. Because you may need to send printed copies to editors who will be making decisions whether to pay you for writing, you will want your copy to be professional-looking. That is only good marketing.

Remember to check before buying any pieces of equipment to make sure they are compatible with each other and with your newspaper's equipment.

Tax Breaks

As you consider buying computer equipment, remember that your Uncle Sam may give you part of the cost of a unit as a gift.

If you are using your computer mainly for your professional writing, you can take advantage of special provisions for business use in the tax code. For computer equipment costing up to $10,000 you may qualify to fully write it off as an expense. Other equipment such as cameras and typewriters used mainly for business also may be deducted as expenses.

Software

Some computers come with the word-processing program you will need to type stories built in or toss in a software disk with such a program as an incentive for purchasers. If not, do not forget to include the price of that software (that is, the instructions or programs that tell the computer what to do) in figuring your cost for using a computer.

When purchasing software, make sure it is compatible with your computer system and consider your individual needs. Some software programs were just made for specific computers.

One of the oldest and most popular word-processing programs, "WordStar," is available for a number of computers. Some applaud its fast editing speed but say that because the program is complex, it takes time to get used to. But that is generally true of word-processing software. Be prepared for a few frustrations while you are learning to use it.

Here is good news for lousy spellers: Spelling programs are available that will check the spelling of each word and let you know if it is not included within the program's dictionary of commonly used words. Most have a 20,000- to

90,000-word dictionary that you can add to with words and names you use regularly. (Typewriters are now also available with spelling checkers.)

The checkers are helpful in catching typographical errors. Spell "the" as "teh" and it will warn you of your error.

You can still, however, manage to let spelling mistakes slip through if you mistakenly write another word found in the dictionary in place of the word you intended. For instance, most checkers will not warn you if you used "effect" when you should have used "affect."

Software such as WordStar and SpellStar can cost you hundreds of dollars. Plan carefully before you invest in software, just as you would before buying a computer.

You can also invest in the relatively new grammar checkers now on the market. But not everyone considers them a helpful aid. Here is what Christopher O'Malley (1985) said about them in "Writing Smarter," published in *Personal Computing* magazine: "Grammar checkers, designed to analyze your writing for conformity to established academic norms of style and grammatical correctness, often misapply a common denominator approach; most professional writers eschew them." But he added, "While they are certainly no substitute for a clear and confident personal writing style they can, in fact, pinpoint consistent misuses and excesses" (p. 54).

Information Retrieval

Even if you cannot get excited about the possibilities of using a computer as a word processor, you will find it opens up a whole new world as a sort of home library, especially if you are writing from a more remote area without a good, large library nearby.

Using your computer to gather information from available databases can save you a tremendous amount of time. No longer do you have to drive to and from your local library and spend hours paging through indexes trying to find the material you want, often to learn it is not available in your local library and you will have to order it through interlibrary loan, which may take weeks. Now you just turn on your computer and search it out.

True, the information collecting is not free. You will usually have to pay to subscribe to a database service and for the connect time it takes to retrieve the information. But you may find the time you save justifies the expense.

Suppose, for instance, an outbreak of food poisoning caused by salmonella bacilli hits your community. You have to prepare a story quickly for that day's deadline.

You know that there had been a recent outbreak of the ailment in nearby Illinois, where a number of people died as a result. But you are hazy on what happened there: How many died? Was the cause ever determined? What has been done to try to prevent a further outbreak? What are the symptoms of the disease?

That kind of background understanding is difficult to get in the time allowed. However, if you have access to an appropriate database, you can round it up through your computer. Just call your database service using the access code it assigned you, connect into the service through your telephone and modem, and search for the needed background.

You might be able to locate helpful stories in major newspapers such as *The Washington Post, The Christian Science Monitor,* or *The New York Times.* You can also check to see what specialized medical sources have to say, such as the information made available through the National Library of Medicine in Bethesda, Maryland. Tell the computer what disease you are interested in and you can get a wide variety of abstracts of research published on the disease.

If you want to save the information, you can preserve it on a disk or print it using your printer.

When you subscribe to a database service, you will probably be given a toll-free number to call for information. Services have hourly rates but just charge for the portion of the hour you have used. Check to see if the company offers lower rates for non-business hours and try to adjust your research time accordingly.

Rates and the type of information offered by services vary tremendously. Think about the kind of information you are most apt to need and make sure you subscribe to the appropriate service.

It can be difficult to locate appropriate services. Here are some of the main ones in which you might be interested.

Because it offers full text of more than 400 newspapers and magazine articles and Associated Press wire-service news (many services just provide abstracts or lists of references), Mead Data Central's Nexis might be a contender. But it is relatively expensive—$50 a month plus a connect time of $35 per hour and a per-search charge that ranges from $6 to $51.

Because of its hefty subscription cost, you might want to see if your local library subscribes to Nexis and conduct your search through the library. The library will probably charge you for using this or other services, but an advantage is that a trained librarian is likely to do the search for you. (Mead Data Central is at 9393 Springboro Pike, Post Office Box 933, Dayton, OH 45401. Phone: 513-865-6800.)

VU/TEXT offers the full text of about 50 newspapers, approximately 180 regional business journals, and a few magazines including *Time.* It also provides news from The Associated Press, PR Newswire, and Business Wire and features from Knight-Ridder Tribune News. Newspaper articles can be searched on a national basis or by state or region.

It was developed by Knight-Ridder Newspapers Inc. as a library service for newspapers and is now used by more newspaper libraries than any other service. Connect-time rates for retrieval start at $105 per hour. Its user's guide is $45.

Because of the relatively high rate, it is unlikely you will want to purchase the service yourself. But some newspapers with VU/TEXT are picking up the bill for writers using the service while working at home for those newspapers. If the newspaper for which you string has VU/TEXT, check to see if the paper is willing for you to use it. Even if you cannot use it for the material just described, your paper may be utilizing VU/TEXT to store its own stories and may be willing to let you use that electronic newspaper library, especially because retrieving its own stories costs only $10 per hour.

Such access to local newspaper files would be of great advantage to a newspaper stringer. Although the newspaper's librarian may be very helpful in mailing you copies of published stories to use as background for your articles, it will take you at least a day to get them in the mail, whereas information available through the electronic storage can be obtained immediately. (VU/TEXT Information Services Inc., 325 Chestnut St., Suite 1300, Philadelphia PA 19106. Phone: 800-323-2940, except Pennsylvania where the number is 215-574-4406.)

Some of the larger information bases used widely by institutions and corporations may ordinarily be too costly for you, but you might be interested in taking advantage of special rates offered by the services for use of certain of their databases during non-business hours.

Knowledge Index, part of Dialog Information Services Inc., provides weekend and evening access to about 70 databases including information on agriculture, business, education, law, and medicine, among other areas. You may find especially useful the PR Newswire and the full text of the Academic American Encyclopedia produced by Grolier Electronic Publishing Inc. Corporate profiles prepared by Standard & Poor's may also provide helpful background for stories.

You can use the service from 6 p.m. through to 5 a.m. the next morning Mondays through Thursdays. Fridays it is available from 6 p.m. to midnight, Saturdays from 8 a.m. to midnight, and Sundays from 3 p.m. to 5 a.m. Monday. All hours are local times.

A one-time fee of $35 also entitles the user to 2 free hours of connect time. The on-line hourly rate for use of the service is $24 per hour. (Dialog Information Services Inc., 3460 Hillview Ave., Palo Alto, CA 94304. Phone: 800-334-2564, except in California where the phone number is 415-858-3810.)

BRS Information Technologies/After Dark, the off-hours service of BRS, offers about 100 databases including the Academic American Encyclopedia. Hours are 6 p.m. your local time to 4 a.m. Eastern time.

The subscription fee of $75 is one time only. On-line costs vary depending on the database being used. They might be as low as $8 an hour or as high as $81 per hour. But note that there is a minimum charge of $12 per month and for some information an additional per citation charge. (BRS, Information Technologies, 8000 Westpark Drive, McLean, VA 22102. Phone: 800-468-0908.)

Here are some other companies you might be interested in.

Dow Jones News-Retrieval—As you might expect from the publisher of *The Wall Street Journal,* this service is especially geared to financial news.

You can get a full text of all the stories in the Journal since 1984 and of business-related articles in more than 200 newspapers and magazines. News from The Associated Press is also available. And current stock prices are among the offerings.

There are various types of members, but the standard membership has a $29.95 basic start-up fee and an $18 annual fee, which is waived for the first year. Basic charges for user time are usually 44¢ per minute for prime time and $2.14 for non-prime. (Dow Jones News-Retrieval, Post Office Box 300, Princeton, NJ 08543-0300. Phone: 800-522-3567 except in New Jersey, Hawaii, Alaska, and Canada where the number is 609-520-8349.)

CompuServe—Among its offerings are Associated Press news from all 50 states and The Washington Post electronic newsletter. It has a "round-the-clock clipping service" that collects articles on any topic you choose and stores them in your "electronic file." The service also offers the Academic American Encyclopedia, Standard & Poor's company profiles, and many consumer services, and it has a Journalism Forum that includes information for free-lance writers. Pricing is complicated. (It takes the company five pages to explain it.) The starter kit is $39.95 and includes $25 worth of usage credit. Connect time ranges from $6 to $15 per hour depending on the time of day and type of modem being used. Additional charges depend on the service being used. (Information Services, Post Office Box 20212, 500 Arlington Centre Blvd., Columbus, OH 43220. Phone: 800-848-8199 except in Ohio where the number is 614-457-0802.)

As an added bonus some of the information services will enable you to perform other special tasks, such as shop via computer and communicate by electronic mail. Or you can even make airline reservations, trade stocks, play games with other subscribers throughout the country, or join special clubs including one for authors.

Some of the services and prices listed here may have been changed before you read this. Ask companies to send you their brochures before subscribing.

Make sure you have appropriate software and computer equipment to handle the information service you plan to use.

The special software needed to allow your computer to receive the information is sometimes supplied by the computer manufacturer or may have to be purchased independently. Some computer manufacturers have also arranged to throw in introductory free time for one of the services.

In looking at appropriate software, you will probably want something that will allow you to interrupt the service's output without otherwise affecting your search. Another welcome convenience is software that enables you to print what is on your screen directly without saving the information on the disk and then printing up the disk's content.

Additional Computer Information

Want more overall information on computer use for writers? A couple of books have been published on the subject. They are *A Writer's Guide to Word Processors* by Shirley Biagi (1984) and *Writing With a Word Processor* by William Zinsser (1983).

Computer Lifestyle

The arrival of computers that have the potential of speeding up and improving the quality of your work places you in the position of making a decision. Do you want to continue using the tried-and-true methods? Or do you want to spend the money and devote the time and aggravation required in deciding what to purchase and mastering the new skills to take advantage of the technology? Many of us have delayed our decision, figuring prices would drop and capabilities of the equipment would improve—and indeed they have. But we may be reaching a plateau with less dramatic changes in prices and word-processing equipment on the horizon. The time may be arriving to make that decision.

Computers have dramatically altered work habits. With the emergence of the new technology, many other types of workers have joined you in working at home for a company located elsewhere. Researchers, programmers, claims processors, marketers—all are now sharing your lifestyle. And with that trend has come a new awareness of the pros and cons of that kind of working environment.

An article in *The Wall Street Journal* by Erik Larson (1985) examined "Working at Home: Is It Freedom Or a Life of Flabby Loneliness?"

The *Journal* article said:

Working at home, linked to the office by a computer terminal, seems like heaven: no commuting, flexible hours, freedom to dress in casual clothes, more time with the family, cheaper and better lunches, higher productivity. It sounds too good to be true, it may be. While most people who have tried 'telecommuting' report real benefits, former nine-to-fivers are also discovering unexpected strains and stresses. (p. 33)

What are some of those strains and stresses? Some of the ones described in the *Journal* article may sound familiar to you.

- Isolation and loneliness because of the lack of interaction with others.
- Fears about being less likely to be promoted.
- The potential for being exploited.
- A tendency to become more of a workaholic because there is always something to do and no reason not to do it.
- Interruptions by friends, relatives, and neighbors who assume that because someone is home, he or she is not really working.
- A losing battle against the bulge because of the easy access to a refrigerator.

The solution? The *Journal* reported that telecommuters are finding ways to cope. Larson wrote: "Most set up an office that can be closed off from the rest of the house. And many create rituals to mark the start and close of the work day" (p. 33).

Other responses included meeting colleagues regularly for lunch, working in the office a couple of days a week, and receiving special attention from managers who try to stay in touch and stroke the remote employee more.

Try some of them out. Set up a separate office, if you do not have one already. You can deduct it for income tax purposes, if the area is used regularly and exclusively for your writing business. A variety of expenses related to the business office, including a percentage of utility bills, insurance, real estate taxes, and mortgage interest can be deducted as expenses associated with your home office. If you decide to purchase computer equipment, you may want a special office space that is more protected than your previous working area.

Set up regular work hours. Do not feel guilty when you stop writing at the end of those hours.

Keep in regular touch with your editor and possibly other writers, if they are nearby, as well as regular sources.

And with your new computer you will be less isolated than you were. With the flick of a switch and a phone call you can be in touch not just with your editor but with information providers, retailers, and other computer users around the country.

THE LIFE OF A STRINGER

As a stringer, you are not alone, although many times you may feel as if you are. Indeed, there are thousands of other stringers across the country sharing your challenges and frustrations, yet with little interaction with other correspondents at their own papers and little or no interaction with stringers working for other publications. Just how many is not known.

The authors of *The News People: A Sociological Portrait of American Journalists and Their Work* looked at the number of U.S. journalists in their 1976 book. They estimated there were 69,500 full-time editorial print and broadcast staffers working at English-language news media in the United States. But they noted the number did not include stringers and other part-time writers.

Of that number, authors John W. C. Johnstone, Edward J. Slawski, and William W. Bowman (1976) said:

> Precisely how many additional persons there are who work for news media on a part-time basis is not known, but what evidence there is suggests that the number may be considerable. One indicator of this is the volume of news stories and articles written by freelancers which are edited by news-media personnel. Some 34.2 percent of the journalists interviewed in the study reported that their job responsibilities included editing or processing news stories or articles prepared by freelancers. From the numbers of such stories they said they had worked on during the previous month, the total flow of such materials into news organizations might run as high as 100,000 pieces per week. (pp. 18–19)

Historical Survey

More helpful figures were available back in the 1940s when research on correspondents was published in a book entitled *Management of Newspaper Correspondents*. Its authors, C. R. F. Smith and Kathryn M. Rheuark (1944), estimated the number at a "quarter of a million correspondents who gather news
of the open-country, the crossroads, and the small towns of the United States
and Canada" (pp. v–vi).

The book, published in 1944, reports on a survey of correspondents and
their background compiled via a magazine called *Folks*, which was put out for
correspondents in the 1930s and 1940s. A cooperative effort of state and regional
press associations, among others, and edited by Smith, it was available to editors
through their press associations and distributed to the correspondents.

Editors of 610 weekly and semi-weekly newspapers in the United States and
Canada who responded to the survey reported having 10,230 correspondents.
An additional 2,441 correspondents were reported by representatives of 80 U.S.
dailies with circulations under 15,000 responding to the survey.

Responses were received from only a small proportion of newspaper editors.
(*Folks* reported in 1938 there were 11,852 weekly and semi-weekly newspapers
in the United States.) But the information collected presents a fascinating profile
of the correspondent at that time.

Of the number reported by the weeklies and semi-weeklies, a meager 11%
were men. The proportion was slightly higher on the dailies—15%.

In those days of World War II, long before the women's lib movement,
the survey shamelessly asked the editors which sex they preferred to hire as
correspondents. The results? Ten percent of the weekly and semi-weekly editors
preferred men, whereas 70% chose women and 20% expressed no preference.
On the dailies, 86% preferred women.

The authors suggested possible explanations for the preference were women's
greater availability for part-time work and the fact that most correspondents
were women. But the reasons cited by one Colorado daily editor were that
"women are best and most reliable" and furthermore will "do much for small
pay."

The editors also had decided preferences as to the occupational backgrounds
they would like to see their correspondents have. Housewives came out on top.
And the runnersup, in order of preference:

- School teachers
- Telephone operators
- Store clerks
- School children

- Preachers

- Farmers

A real find, the book suggests, combines the top two backgrounds.

> Perhaps some of the most successful correspondents are women who have been school teachers but who have married local men and now reside in the community. They usually have the ability to write, are interested in gathering the news, are permanent, and on the whole are more fair-minded than life-long residents of the neighborhood. However, it is not always possible to find such a person in the community. (p. 23)

Preachers, on the other hand, did not always share that same reputation for fairness. The men of the cloth came burdened with an occupational hazard. "The preacher is able to gather the news and usually has some ability in writing it, but one complaint is that he mixes news and religion" (p. 23) stated the book.

But the authors conceded, "The natural ability of the correspondent, rather than his profession or status in life, should be the guide to his selection" (p. 23).

Think your pay as a stringer is dismally low? Actually, the situation today is looking up, as the opening sentence on the book's chapter on "Correspondent Compensation" indicates: "Should correspondents be paid?"

The answer was apparently mixed. The survey found that 75% of the American weeklies and semi-weeklies that responded and 47% of the Canadian weeklies and semi-weeklies paid their correspondents. Of U.S. dailies under 15,000 circulation, 85% paid them.

By far the most popular method of payment was by the inch, and the most common reward was 5¢ per inch. Other methods of payment reported were by the column, item, or line and by the week, month, quarter, or year.

Cash prizes were given out by some papers for the best story of the week, the greatest amount of news, and dependability. Sound good? Not when you consider that sometimes this bonanza was in lieu of salary.

Then again, remuneration might be in the form of free want ads, subscriptions, movie passes, or county fair tickets. And some reported community pride was payment. But would local bankers accept it as a deposit?

Some editors encouraged their correspondents to sell subscriptions, with typical commissions at 50% for new orders and 25% for renewals. And some editors even encouraged their stringers to solicit ads.

Editors were also asked about their correspondents' shortcomings. Many an editor supervising correspondents today could empathize with the editors naming their stringers' most common faults more than 40 years ago. Here they are, in order of the number of times they were cited.

- Write up same people too often
- Overlook or cannot judge real news
- Too many visiting items
- Don't know how to write a news story
- Don't send copy in on time
- Bad grammar
- Can't read their writing
- Don't get names correctly
- Poor spelling
- Not dependable
- News items too short
- News items too long

About 75% of the editors reported that they attempted to carry out a training program to help correspondents overcome their shortcomings. The authors also reported that extension divisions of a few state universities had offered news writing courses for correspondents, at an average cost of $10. The University of Minnesota even offered a correspondence correspondents course. Many newspapers used regular house organs or occasional bulletins to help train correspondents.

And many papers made the publication *Folks* available to their correspondents. The monthly *Folks*, the Helpmate of the Newspaper Correspondents, initially appeared in December 1937. It was a 16-page, 3 1/2-by-6-inch miniature magazine illustrated with cartoons and pictures. According to a brochure promoting the publication, its aim was "to help. . . correspondents in a nice way—without preaching too much, without over-use of the teacher-pupil method, striving always and above all to make them like their work and to be loyal to their home newspaper."

Correspondents would send in samples of their news items for analysis, and errors would be pointed out. Suggestions for gathering and writing news, style hints, and stories about correspondents were reported to have been among the favorite features in *Folks*.

One *Folks* article published in 1938 estimated that if a week's worth of newspaper columns written by U.S. correspondents were pasted together end to end, they would extend for more than 25 miles.

The authors of *Management of Newspaper Correspondents* reported on the high regard with which newspaper editors viewed the valuable role performed by the correspondent. Take this tribute, for instance, from John A. Boyer, editor of the *News Chronicle* in Scott City, Kansas. "The editor who does not wake up to the real value of correspondence as the backbone of his paper," he said, "is due for a rude awakening when the going gets tough" (p. vi).

But despite such appreciation of their role, *Management of Newspaper Correspondents* stated, "No department in newspaper-making has been more neglected by researchers and textbook writers" (p. viii). That was true in 1944, and it still seems to be true today. My research uncovered very little that had been written for or about correspondents. Despite their numbers and significance as a news-gathering force, they seem to have been largely overlooked.

Because of the lack of information available on stringers, I have begun to survey individuals taking part in correspondents' workshops I have been asked to conduct. The number questioned at this point is very small, but you may find it interesting to compare your situation with the responses of some stringers working for Wisconsin papers.

Backgrounds of Stringers

The 41 Wisconsin stringers questioned brought a wide variety of backgrounds to their task. Twenty-five reported having had previous writing experience. For some, that experience included full-time journalism employment. For instance, one had been the editor and publisher of a small weekly, and another was working as the news director of a local radio station.

Many were stringing for several papers, with some writing for as many as five papers. Some combined stringing with other free-lance forms of writing such as poetry, fiction, or magazine articles.

Thirty-two reported they were also employed at other jobs, some of them part time.

Among their other occupations were working as a dairy farmer, artist, teacher, university lecturer, proofreader, secretary, locksmith, and director of alumni relations for a college.

Seventeen reported having had formal writing training.

As is happening elsewhere, untrained individuals without full-time journalism experience are working as stringers for smaller papers. But often the larger dailies use many stringers who are working full time for smaller newspapers or for broadcast stations or have other journalism background.

The stringers questioned ranged in age from 23 to 73. Almost half were in their 30s or early 40s. Here is the breakdown of their ages.

20–24—2

25–29—5

30–34—8

35–39—4
40–44—5
45–49—2
50–54—5
55–59—2
60–64—1
65–69—2
70–74—2

Three did not report their age.

Of those attending workshops, 10 of the 41 working as stringers had been writing for less than 1 year. It is probable that the more inexperienced were more likely to attend a training workshop. However, there often does seem to be a rapid turnover among stringers for varying reasons. Among them might be frustration involved in attempting to do something for which one has not been trained, poor pay, and a new job that makes it difficult to find time to string.

Eleven others of those surveyed were fairly new to the job, having been a stringer for from 1 to 3 years.

On the other hand, one individual had worked as a stringer for 46 years and another for 34 years.

Number and Types of Stories

Of those who gave an estimate of the number of bylined stories they write per month, 10 estimated 1 to 4, 9 estimated 5 to 8, 8 estimated 9 to 12, and 4 said more than 12.

As for their responsibilities, 29 reported they regularly cover municipal government meetings, 21 regularly cover school board meetings, and 11 regularly cover police news. Of the 41 respondents, 34 said they write regularly on feature subjects.

Many reported they mainly generated their own ideas for stories.

Compensation

Of those who responded to the questions, 17 stringers said they thought they were paid adequately for their work, and 14 believed they were not. In fact, many thought they were probably not earning minimum wage. Thirteen thought they were not making that wage, whereas 18 said they were.

Methods of payment varied tremendously. They included payment by the story, the inch, and time spent as well as a regular salary.

Three of the stringers estimated they made under $50 a month from stringing whereas on the other end of the scale one in their midst estimated the monthly income at a total of $1,500 to $2,000. Five estimated they made $400 or more a month. About half of those who provided an estimate of their remuneration earned between $100 and $400 monthly.

Low pay seems to be a sore point for many stringers. One anonymous stringer spoke out on the subject in a letter to the editor of the *Columbia Journalism Review* (Anonymous, 1982). "Sure, reporters are underpaid," the stringer wrote. "But if you've never been a rural stringer for a big-city paper, you don't know what underpaid means" (p. 65).

The writer, who was paid at the rate of $1.37 per inch for articles set in wide-column measure and $1.07 for narrow columns, described how he or she had spent 6 hours on a story covering the county legislature. But the story was cut to just over 2 inches and the stringer's gross was $3.08.

However, the writer added, "It isn't all bad" noting he or she could make $32.52 an hour writing obituaries.

Although the responses of the stringers for Wisconsin papers indicate many believe they are not being adequately compensated for their efforts, a number of them respond their main reason for stringing is to earn extra money.

Reason for Stringing

However, for a number of others money is not the main incentive. Reasons for stringing included responses like: "to stay in training for journalism while temporarily pursuing another line of work," "to improve writing skills and observation skills," "to fulfill a need for personal growth," "for the joy of writing," and "personal satisfaction; to continue to use my education."

In fact, one stringer, asked to indicate in a priority order the role various factors played in his decision to string, very clearly indicated the lowly role money played. He ranked four factors in this way:

1. to gain experience to help land a full-time journalism job
2. to develop writing skills
3. to be involved in what is happening in my community
10. to earn extra money

(Incidentally, he was one of the stringers who believed he was receiving less than minimum wage.)

For some it seems to be a hobby they enjoy pursuing and are glad that someone is willing to pay them for that enjoyment. After all, how many hobbies are there that do not end up costing you money?

But the fact that so many are willing to contribute stories at such a low minimum hourly rate probably means that editors are not likely to increase the rate of compensation significantly. They have little incentive to do so when some of the most conscientious and dedicated writers are willing to do it for the love of it.

With such low remuneration, it is a rare stringer who is able to support him or herself on a stringer's pay. Although you might indeed write for a larger paper that pays you $150 for a feature story, it would be tough to crank out enough articles to make a living at it. And usually you would be without the benefits enjoyed by full-time employees, such as health insurance, Social Security contributions, and paid vacations.

Because stringers tend to be scattered all over the paper's circulation area, they are unlikely to get together in an organized effort to request more pay. The only time they may see each other is at the training sessions and recognition dinners papers hold for their stringers.

Multiple Sales

When I started conducting stringer workshops, I learned many stringers had found what was to me a surprising solution for helping to make their efforts pay off. They were stringing not just for one but as many as five different papers and frequently giving exactly the same story to a number of papers.

For me that was surprising because when I was an editor supervising stringers in New York state, I would not have wanted to pay for the same story run by other papers, unless perhaps it were routine, straightforward information such as an obituary or an announcement of a speech. But the editors directing these stringers seem willing to pay even for feature stories used by papers catering to readers in the same circulation area.

My first reaction, I must confess, was to question whether what the stringers were doing with their multiple sales was professional. But having learned how widespread the practice was in Wisconsin and the stringers' rationale for their marketing techniques, I have altered my viewpoint somewhat.

Indeed it is difficult to make a reasonable hourly wage writing for one paper. As one stringer put it, he saw himself as a news service. If many papers run the same Associated Press story as other papers, then why shouldn't stringers be paid by a number of papers for the same story?

But on the other hand, good editors of competitive papers generally like to have their own reporters cover news of their local area that is important enough to run on the wire. They want to beat out the competitors in their coverage of their circulation area, and you cannot do that when you are running the same story as those competitors.

However, editors would rather have the story than miss out on the news altogether. As a practical matter, if receiving a non-exclusive story is the only way they can get the news, that is better than nothing.

I would think an editor might either attempt to get a stringer to cover stories for that paper exclusively or try to find another at least equally competent stringer who will.

But if you as a stringer can get several editors to buy the same story and reap the rewards, more power to you. In many cases it is probably a testimony to your abilities. Your editor may not be able to get elsewhere exclusive stories that measure up to the quality of your articles.

Professionally, however, you may decide it is best not to also offer your stories to the competition. But that professional question is not likely to arise when you are submitting the stories to newspapers in other geographic areas or to magazines. Those publications are not competing for the same readers and therefore even the most competitive editor is not likely to be unhappy about such sales.

In fact, do not forget about such publications as possible sources of revenue. Many local stories you have written might be of interest to people living elsewhere. You can learn what magazine and some newspaper editors want by checking *Writer's Market*, published annually by Writer's Digest Books (Neff & Cinnamon, 1989).

Legal Rights

Legally, unless you have made an agreement to the contrary, your stories written as a free-lance stringer for newspapers are yours to resell. Under federal copyright legislation, in the absence of any agreement to the contrary, it is assumed that you are the owner of that right.

Full-time newspaper staffers do not enjoy that same right. Works "made for hire" written by staff employees are in the hands of the person or institution for whom they were created.

On the other hand, if you are the newspaper's employee, you are entitled to benefits such as the paper's payment of part of your Social Security cost. (As a free lancer you have to pay a whopping 15.3% of your net income over $400 as a self-employment tax unless you had other income of $51,300 or more which was subject to Social Security tax.)

Questions have arisen over at what point a writer ceases to be an independent contractor and becomes, in effect, an employee of the paper.

"There is no pat answer for this," said Mary Sepucha (personal communication), director of labor relations with the American Newspaper Publishers Association about the difference between staff and free-lance status. It is a "balancing test," she said of the decisions in which the issue has been raised. Among the factors that might be weighed are:

- Does the editor assign stories?
- Does the writer use newspaper equipment or space?
- Is the writer paid a salary, compensated for the story, or paid by the amount of space filled by his or her stories?
- Does the writer use an identification card issued by the newspaper?
- Does the writer work a regular schedule under supervision?
- Is the writer free to accept or reject story assignments?
- Is the writer free to work for competing organizations?

The answers to these questions are likely to determine whether you are an employee of the paper. Some editors hesitate to assign stories for fear it might tip the balance and turn you into a newspaper staffer.

Stringers concerned about preserving their right as independent contractors to resell their stories complain that right has been violated because The Associated Press wire service is running their stories published in papers for which they string without their receiving additional compensation.

The Associated Press is a non-profit cooperative of member newspapers and broadcasters. Those members have an obligation to feed the wire with newsworthy stories their reporters have written and other AP members might be interested in using. And AP staffers can go through their member newspapers and use stories produced by their reporters.

Because staff reporters are producing work made for hire, their stories can be used by AP with no compensation and without any legal difficulty.

But copyright specialist Ellen M. Kozak (personal communication), a Milwaukee attorney, said if the wire uses a stringer's story without further compensation, that usage is clearly a violation of the stringer's rights as set forth in the copyright law.

An AP spokeswoman, asked about the stringers' complaints, suggested the decisions to use the stories for the wire may have been made by the newspaper editors. She said when stories are run by the wire exactly as they appeared originally in the newspaper, those stories have been transmitted to the AP by newspaper personnel. A wire staffer using the information from a published newspaper alters the words, she said.

Ms. Kozak, a stringer herself for *USA Today*, said part of the problem is that AP is unable to tell which stories are written by free lancers in many newspapers.

She suggested stringers' work might be identified by a copyright symbol or some type of credit line that makes it clear what the source of the information is. Such a label would serve as a warning to the AP not to use the story without compensating the writer.

She cautioned that trying to protect their rights is a touchy job for stringers. Attempts at changes to try to get additional compensation for the stringers may get the local paper in trouble with AP or the stringer in trouble with the local paper, she warned. She suggested the stringers might want to talk to their editors about the problem but said the editors might just decide they would rather not deal with someone they view as a troublemaker and stop buying their stories.

Such issues facing stringers suggest there is perhaps a need for an organized effort that could help them with concerns such as this that are difficult for them to address individually. Perhaps someday there will be a national organization of stringers.

And it is likely more may become involved in union activities. At the *Village Voice* in New York City free lancers are represented by a union, which has helped spell out work rules on payment rates, benefits, and other matters. A group of stringers at the *Philadelphia Inquirer* successfully petitioned the Philadelphia office of the National Labor Relations Board to rule that eligible stringers who covered the suburbs for the *Inquirer* were employees with the right to organize a union.

Taking Photographs

In addition to selling your work to several publications, you might also want to pick up some more money by taking pictures to illustrate your stories. A further advantage is you will increase the chances of getting good play for your newspaper story if you have an exceptional picture to go with it. Some features, like personality profiles, cry out for a picture. If you do not take a picture of that interview subject, your editor may send out a full-time photographer to do so.

Here is what one newspaper, *The Milwaukee Journal*, says it is looking for in a picture, according to its guide for correspondents:

> We need clear, well-composed, well-lighted pictures. The camera must be fo-
> cused, the subjects carefully spaced, and shadows must not obscure faces. A
> common fault of photographers is the reluctance to get close to people to strive
> for 'tight' composition. . . . Scenery is nice, and we wouldn't want to prevent you
> from sending us your best pictures of pretty scenes. But, most of the time, pictures
> of people are more interesting than pictures of things.

Check with your editor to see how the developing work should be handled. *The Milwaukee Journal*, for instance, would prefer to receive processed negatives and have them printed in their own lab.

Do not forget to provide information for captions. Identify all recognizable people.

Some papers like and have the space to use picture stories. "We love them," the *Journal* guide says. "If you come upon an event which, you feel, could be told in pictures, please go to it. The key to successful picture stories is variety: a variety of camera angles, of expressions, of closeups and overall pictures. The result could well be a layout on the state news page, or even a full picture page."

Pictures can be crucial in making a later sale of your feature to a magazine. The magazine office is likely to be in another part of the country, and few magazine editors are able to afford to send a photographer to far-flung parts of the country to take pictures to illustrate your article. If you cannot take a picture yourself, consider hiring a photographer to do so.

Productivity

Another important consideration in making a living wage is effective use of your time. It is very easy to procrastinate and fritter away time when you are working as a free lancer. Be conscious of how you spend your time and how much you accomplish. Discipline is crucial. You may want to set aside certain hours of the day that you will devote to stringing. But you will have to remain flexible—collecting information for every story the paper needs will not always fit within those hours.

Create a weekly goal for yourself. Decide, for instance, that you will write one substantial feature story each week. Consider aiming for one good, solid in-depth piece each month in addition to regular stories. You might also aim to turn in a couple of hard news stories each day. If you are not conscious of your production, you are likely to get to the end of the month with a much smaller string of stories than you had realized.

The more you do, the more productive you will become. Not only will you be able to write more quickly and research stories more efficiently. You will find that one piece will lead to follow-up stories and one interview or event will lead to multiple ideas for other pieces.

And if you work on a regular basis, cranking out news starts to seem effortless. But go for a couple of weeks without stringing, and the task can seem much more difficult.

Do not let the little frustrations that accompany any job, including stringing, interfere with your productivity. Sitting off in your own little work world, it is very easy to waste valuable time stewing over what you have perceived as shabby treatment. Your story was cut, your most cherished sentence was edited, your article was buried amid the classified ads, your editor was too busy to talk to you. All of this goes with the territory you cover.

Professionalism

Be professional in your approach to your job—and that means understanding the needs of your paper and the problems of your editor.

Realize that a large number of stories have to be cut to enable them to fit on a page. Learn from the changes in your stories and the way they are played. Yes, editors sometimes make mistakes and edit errors into your copy or fail to appreciate the news value of the article you have submitted. But their decisions are generally based on many years of experience. Your copy is often improved by their editing, and perhaps you were too close to the story to understand its true news value.

Also remember that your editor is doing the job under great deadline pressure. Sometimes his or her judgment may be less than perfect because of those time constraints. And at times your editor may not be able to take a moment to talk to you because of those looming deadlines.

One of your annoyances may have been what you have viewed as trespassing on your turf. The complaint was expressed by the letter writer to the *Columbia Journalism Review* referred to earlier who wrote "the rule is: woe to the stringer, who, when big stories come along, is passed over. For the organized crimes, for the multiple deaths in accidents, even for the little stories that are so odd they're big, a reporter is sent down from The City. A real reporter" (p. 65).

The extent to which this happens varies considerably from one paper to another. Many of you, no doubt, have covered organized crimes, multiple accident deaths and the big little story, especially if you have been a stringer for the same paper for a number of years and won your editor's trust.

You have perhaps more often found yourself pushed aside when the story angle gets into one of the specialty beat areas, such as medicine or the environment. Then the paper may send in the specialist reporter to work the story, but the same thing can happen to a full-time reporter who is asked to step aside and turn the story over to the specialist. Specialty beats have been created for more complex areas in which it is especially helpful to be an expert knowledgeable about the subject.

Furthermore, a good editor will appreciate that writers are better at covering some types of stories than others. For instance, some have a stylish, colorful way of writing that can bring extra impact to a feature story. Others are tireless diggers who can produce a good investigative story from the most elusive material.

Understanding those differences, the perceptive editor may summon a full-time reporter to cover a significant story that comes up in your area because that reporter's skills are better suited for the task. And yes, sometimes you may just not have had enough experience to handle a difficult story and reinforcements will be called in.

If so, do not get upset. Offer whatever assistance you can to the reporter, who is probably not as familiar with the area as you are. Sometimes the editor will ask you to produce a joint story with that reporter. You can learn a lot from working with a pro.

If you disagree with the way something is handled or do not understand something, talk it over with your editor. For many, the learning possibilities the stringing job offers can be its greatest reward. Learn from the experiences of the newspaper's staff and communicate effectively with those professionals. Remember that they and you are both trying to attain the same goal—to meet the informational needs of your readers and thus provide a valuable public service.

Understand the role you are expected to perform and do it to the best of your ability. And have a good grasp of your own needs and take them into account in deciding on your priorities. Do you need the money from stringing to support yourself and your family? If so, look for a lot of stories you can effectively write up after interviewing only one source.

Do you, on the other hand, not need to depend on the money you derive from stringing? Do you have a desire to extend your investigative reporting talents to the limit? Do you want to make a difference in your community? Watch for the issue-oriented stories in which you can help the paper serve its important role of community watchdog. They can be very time-consuming but exceedingly satisfying contributions.

There are basic types of coverage your editor is likely to want you to handle. But beyond these demands you will probably be relatively free to generate your own ideas for stories.

Each stringer brings his or her own set of needs, skills, and interests to the task. Wondrously, the job offers unlimited possibilities to carve out a role uniquely suited to you.

STRINGERS AT WORK

The job of a stringer varies as much as the individual filling it. It is yours to make of what you will, once you have taken care of responding to your paper's basic needs. As the previous chapter indicates, editors will have to give you a fair amount of freedom or risk turning you into a regular employee entitled to all of the benefits of the rest of the staff.

It may evolve into an hour-a-week task or the equivalent of a full-time job plus overtime. Some stringers simply pass along occasional club news to their papers, others are top-notch investigative reporters devoting long and difficult hours to their work. And for some it has become a family affair with spouses helping out in monitoring police scanners, lining up interviews, and sometimes even covering meetings that the other spouse is unable to attend because of a time conflict.

Eleanor Yoder: A Stringer, Day and Night

Done conscientiously, the work is time-consuming and ever a challenge. For an idea of what is involved in first-rate professional stringing, meet a veteran correspondent who does it right. Her dedication to her profession is much-appreciated by her editors and might serve as an example for stringers everywhere.

Eleanor Yoder (personal communication), who lives in Ephrata, Pennsylvania, specializes in covering breaking news stories in northern Lancaster County.

She is on top of what the police are involved with in her region throughout the day.

Her turf is the gently rolling countryside of the fertile Pennsylvania Dutch region of southeastern Pennsylvania. She is responsible for covering her area for a total of four daily papers in Lancaster and Reading. And she works for 30 hours a week as social and church editor of a weekly in Ephrata.

Most of her stringing work is done from her home on a neat-looking, Norman Rockwellish street in the midst of Ephrata where visitors are greeted by three dogs and a cat.

Only a small percent of correspondents approach the task with the diligence of an Eleanor Yoder. She is making a contribution that is a valuable service to the community she has come to know so well over the years.

Police news is her first love, and she is determined not to miss any of the goings-on in her area. "I enjoy working with the police," she said, her speech somewhat flavored by the Pennsylvania Dutch accent characteristic of the area.

A police scanner allowing her to listen in on the communications of local law enforcement officers is chattering away in the background of the Yoder household day and night. She even has a scanner on both floors so she will not miss a word if she needs to go upstairs for a moment. She has found most incidents happen at night.

Ms. Yoder goes about her business, yet can suddenly tune into the information on the scanner if a newsworthy incident arises. If she hears something that has story possibilities, she usually waits about an hour, then phones authorities for the specifics. She delays calling because she has learned it takes police officers a while to get back to the office and file their reports.

But she is not satisfied with just picking up news she hears on the police broadcasts. In addition, she makes numerous calls throughout the day to check on what is going on. "I do think the most important thing for correspondents is to make regular calls," she said.

During a typical day, if nothing unusual is happening, she might call the state police barracks in Ephrata four times, the Ephrata borough police three times, the Lancaster County Control (which dispatches police, firemen, and ambulances) twice, the turnpike state police twice, and the local hospital three times.

She has arranged with police chiefs of various smaller areas she does not contact on a regular basis to call her when they have handled newsworthy incidents.

Because she is working for morning and afternoon papers, her first call is at about 6:30 a.m. and her last at 11 p.m. She is very aware of her editors' needs and tries to call in her stories as early as possible because she knows how difficult it is for editors to have all their news arriving on deadline.

For Ms. Yoder the job continues 7 days a week, day and night. "The only thing with this job is that your time isn't really your own," she said. Even

Christmas Eve was working time as she called in a story on a fire in a mobile home and a traffic fatality.

When she must be away from her home, she tries as much as possible to arrange to do so at a time that is not near a deadline. If she does for some reason have to be away, for instance when she goes on vacation, she lets her editors know so they can make other arrangements for picking up the news.

Although she has to plan her activities around making her regular checks, she has found those calls do not take long if nothing is happening. A typical week might yield about 20 police stories. And each call to the local hospital generally turns up one new birth.

Sometimes her routine checks will lead to information about incidents outside her assigned area of coverage. If so, she does not write up the story but does notify her editor of the incident so someone else can do the story. She gets paid for the news tip.

In collecting her information, Ms. Yoder has learned over the years to look for interesting details. Her first coverage of a fire was part of that learning experience.

She called in the story about a space heater exploding and causing the fire. The news staff member taking the information asked her if anyone was in the room. That was one thing she had forgotten to ask about. A follow-up question to authorities resulted in the information that a baby had been in the room. The detail was added and the headline reported that a baby had escaped injury in the disaster. "You have to ask enough questions," Ms. Yoder emphasized.

To make sure that she asked all the appropriate questions, she decided to use memory joggers, which she highly recommends, especially for beginning correspondents. She lists questions on index cards, which she can quickly refer to as she talks to the authorities. For instance, her card for checking on a fire would include questions such as when and where the fire took place, what was burned, which companies responded to the fire, what pieces of equipment were used, how many firemen were involved, were any of them injured, were any people or pets at the scene when the fire erupted, and how high were the flames. She keeps her memory joggers short so that she can quickly and easily scan the card without interfering with her conversation with her sources.

With automobile accidents she has learned that in addition to the usual questions about the circumstances of the accident, it is a good idea to ask where those involved were coming from and going to.

She has not found it helpful to go to the scene of accidents. She wants to get her information from the authorities, and at the scene, law enforcement officers are likely to be busy talking to the individuals involved in the accident.

Although Ms. Yoder has a camera, she leaves pictures of the accident scenes to free-lance photographers in the area.

Occasionally she has run into the kind of problems with sources so familiar to many correspondents. A police representative will say everything is quiet when it really isn't, or a police report may be a week late in being filed. When she had problems with late reports, she decided to complain because a week-late report is of no use to a newspaper.

She also goes to three or four government meetings a month and picks up information on several others by phone. "I take many more notes than needed," she said. As the meeting progresses, she puts numerals next to her notes to indicate the order of importance of the issue involved. This helps her organize her thoughts quickly, a skill that is especially important because she often has to dictate her story on deadline without having time to write it first.

Another trick she has learned is to use a tape recorder at meetings, but only during the time when visitors are given a chance to speak their minds. She wants to make sure she gets those quotes. "If I want to use a direct quote, I want to make certain I use it exactly," she said. As she tapes that quote, she jots down in her notes the number of the section of the tape where it has been recorded so later she can find it quickly. But she does not trust the tape recorder implicitly. She continues to take notes as if she did not have it on, in case something should go wrong.

She still provides some news for the social pages of papers for which she strings but has seen big changes in those sections over the years. Now, she said, they cut back the club news so much that sometimes she thinks it's not worthwhile to submit those items, but she does not turn down such stories.

And then there is the annual cow-milking contests, greased-pig chases, and other events of the Ephrata farm show. "That's sort of a hectic event," she said.

Here, too, she has learned her lesson over the years. "My normal inclinations are to head for the front row," said the intrepid reporter. But after being splattered by a cow and having her foot trampled on by a pig, she learned to pick a different spot.

She also writes an occasional feature but has found it difficult to do that kind of more creative writing in recent years in the wake of some serious family problems. Yet through these tragedies she continued her regular reporting and service to the newspapers. She makes her calls no matter what else is happening in her life.

Like many female stringers, she decided to become a correspondent while raising a family and looking for work she could do from her home. She started when the youngest of her four sons was 8 and the oldest was 13. Because about 95% of her work is done over the phone, she could do her job and still be at home to meet her children's needs.

She started stringing after responding to an ad for the position in the newspaper. "As soon as I saw that, I knew that was for me," she remembered. But, she added, "I don't think my husband was overjoyed." Yet today he makes helpful contributions to the job, jotting down information he hears over the scanner while she is away from home.

Although Ms. Yoder had some previous journalism background working for her high school paper and taking journalism classes, most of what she has learned is through on-the-job experience.

She urges those new to the job to learn by looking carefully at the versions of the stories they submit and noting how they compare with the way the articles appear in the paper.

Job satisfaction rather than monetary rewards seems to be a major incentive for her. She gets paid by the inch and receives bonuses for stories as well as payments for news tips. But she will never get rich stringing. "There are a lot of jobs that pay a lot better than this one," she said.

Ms. Yoder has turned down several offers for full-time employment with papers, including an offer years ago to work as an obituary writer. At that time she wanted to stay at home with her children, and she decided her stringer's job with the variety it offered might be more interesting. But she wishes she had the pension and other benefits a full-time position would have afforded.

"I enjoy the work," she said of stringing. "I've met some marvelous people. I like the reporters. They're interesting people." And she enjoys seeing her stories in the pages of the papers.

Nonetheless, she welcomes the breaks from her stringing responsibilities. "I love vacations," she said. "We go out in the boondocks. There's no monitors, no phones."

Options for Stringers

Some full-time news staffers have switched over to the life of a stringer, allowing them to enjoy the freedom of setting their own hours and picking the scenic spot where they would like to set up their writing business. A former Associated Press writer living on the Oregon coast decided to string for the *Salem States-man-Journal,* as did a retired daily newspaper editor from California. An editor on the state desk at *The Milwaukee Journal* chose to use her retirement years to return to the stringing job in the lake area of Wisconsin she had enjoyed before joining the *Journal* as a full-time staffer.

The relative flexibility stringing offers is no doubt a lure for many, but editors caution against writers hoping to earn a living at it. "If you want to do it on a full-time basis, stringing is not the way to go," said Gene Quinn (personal communication), suburban editor of the *Chicago Tribune.*

But for the person looking for a fascinating way to earn some extra money during retirement years or while holding down another job, or for inexperienced journalists hoping to build up a portfolio that will help them land a full-time job, stringing may be an exciting and rewarding challenge.

And the jobs are out there in many regions. The state editor for the *Sacra-*

mento Bee, Loretta Kalb (personal communication), for instance, said she is always on the lookout for good stringers, but "it's just real tough" to find qualified and willing individuals in many towns. She has had difficulty locating people willing to devote the time and energy needed for a job that does not pay enough to allow them to live on what they make from their writing. She looks for those who like doing it and do not need it to put bread on the table. An attorney, for instance, is among her stringers. Among her past stringers was a pit boss at a gambling casino.

Stringing opportunities are generally especially good in areas that are too far away from the main office of a daily for the paper's reporters to cover them routinely, yet close enough that the newspaper's staff consider them part of the region in which they would like the paper to circulate.

And in recent years, stringing opportunities seem to be increasing for those living in the suburbs of larger cities as metropolitan papers push to increase their circulations in those often wealthier areas, frequently in competition against the local suburban papers. Because they are trying to cover so many municipalities for the various editions they are putting out, the metros are hiring stringers to help get the job done, as are the local suburban papers struggling to protect their turf against the metros.

The Chicago Tribune, for instance, has recently been relying more heavily on suburban stringers as part of its attempt to extend its coverage into target areas and report on 263 municipalities. It now has about three dozen stringers providing news of suburbia.

Amy Krieger Rippis (1988), who has herself worked as a correspondent, reported on what she sees as the change in the use of part-time reporters in *The Quill,* published by the Society of Professional Journalists. "In these days of labor-intensive 'community journalism,' a nitty-gritty brand of reporting that is practiced by even large metro dailies, the hiring of part-timers is a growing national trend," she wrote. "Somebody has to go to all of those school board meetings, and part-timers do it more cheaply" (p. 29).

She reported that correspondents are nothing new at the paper where she was a correspondent, *The Record* in Hackensack, New Jersey, located in one of the most densely populated parts of the nation. But the breed of those writers has changed significantly in the last 10 years. "Correspondents then were more likely to be moonlighters, housewives, school teachers and public relations professionals who wanted to keep a hand in journalism and earn some extra cash" (p. 29), she wrote.

"The correspondents corps, which numbers about 30, is now almost entirely composed of journalists making a step toward what they hope will be a full-time career" (p. 29). Many are recent college graduates with little or no journalism experience who had a hard time landing their first job. Others could have had a full-time reporting job elsewhere but preferred to work in that area of New

Jersey because of its proximity to Manhattan. Quite a few have used the corre-spondent job as a stepping stone to successful jobs elsewhere, including positions at the *Los Angeles Times, Time,* and *Business Week.*

The makeup of suburban stringers at the *Chicago Tribune* appears to be similar. "Most are younger folks trying to build a portfolio," Quinn said, noting many move on to full-time jobs at smaller papers.

A large proportion of papers of all sizes use stringers to some extent, including *The Washington Post, USA Today,* and *The New York Times,* which circulate nationwide. You might also be able to arrange a stringing job with one of the news magazines. *Newsweek,* for instance, which hires stringers for tips and background information as well as stories, has at least one in each state.

Even in the most remote areas throughout this large country there are stringers helping to preserve the happenings of today as the history of tomorrow for their communities. I even met one such stringer in the wilderness of Alaska, far from the nearest roads. He signaled the Anchorage-to-Fairbanks train I was riding to stop at the milestone near the spot where he had homesteaded. His address was the milestone number of the railroad line where his mail was dropped off, his beat for the *Anchorage Daily News* was the wilderness in which he lived.

These thousands of stringers are helping to string together a patchwork picture of their United States that is a very different and more complex fabric than would exist without them. Their craftsmanship preserves some of the finest and most noteworthy bits and pieces of their far-flung communities that together make up the texture of the American way of life.

For the United States is not just New York and Boston, Chicago and San Francisco, and the other publishing centers. It is Ephrata and Oshkosh, Albert-ville and Batesville, Ickesburg and Kecksburg, and all the other little burgs where news is breaking every day. And the rest of the world knows about such communities and what is happening there thanks to the work of their stringers.

REFERENCES

Books

Agee, W. K., Ault, P. H., & Emery, E. (1983). *Reporting and writing the news.* New York: Harper & Row.

American Bar Association. (1980). *Law and the courts.* Chicago: ABA Press.

Berner, R. T. (1979). *Language skills for journalists.* Boston: Houghton Mifflin.

Biagi, S. (1984). *A writer's guide to word processors.* Englewood Cliffs, NJ: Prentice-Hall.

Brooks, B. S., & Pinson, J. L. (1989). *Working with words: A concise guide for media editors and writers.* New York: St. Martin's Press.

Burken, J. L. (1979). *Introduction to reporting* (2nd ed.). Dubuque, IA: Wm. C. Brown.

Callihan, E. L. (1979). *Grammar for journalists.* Radnor, PA: Chilton Book.

Dennis, E. E., & Ismach, A. H. (1981). *Reporting processes and practices: Newswriting for today's readers.* Belmont, CA: Wadsworth.

Denniston, L. W. (1980). *The reporter and the law: Techniques of covering the courts.* New York: Hastings House.

French, C. W., & Goldstein, N. (Eds.). (1988). *The Associated Press stylebook and libel manual.* New York: The Associated Press.

Hough, G. A. (1984). *News writing* (3rd ed.). Boston: Houghton Mifflin.

Johnstone, J. W. C., Slawski, E. J., & Bowman, W. W. (1976). *The news people: A sociological portrait of American journalists and their work.* Urbana, IL: University of Illinois Press.

Kessler, L., & McDonald, D. (1984). *When words collide: A journalist's guide to grammar and style.* Belmont, CA: Wadsworth.

Mencher, M. (1984). *News reporting and writing* (3rd ed.). Dubuque, IA: Wm. C. Brown.

Metzler, K. (1989). *Creative interviewing: The writer's guide to gathering information by asking questions* (2nd ed.). Englewood Cliffs, NJ: Prentice-Hall.

Neff, G. T., & Cinnamon, D. (Eds.). (1989). *1990 writer's market: Where & how to sell what you write.* Cincinnati: Writer's Digest Books.

Smith, C. R. F., & Rheuark, K. M. (1944), *Management of newspaper correspondents.* Baton Rouge, LA: Louisiana State University Press.

Ward, H. H. (1985). *Professional newswriting.* San Diego, CA: Harcourt Brace Jovanovich.

Wilhoit, G. C., Weaver, D., & Gray, R. (1986). *The American journalist: A portrait of U.S. news people and their work.* Bloomington, IN: Indiana University Press.

Zinsser, W. K. (1983). *Writing with a word processor.* New York: Harper & Row.

Court Cases

Anderson v. Liberty Lobby, 477 U.S. 242 (1986).

Associated Press v. Walker, 388 U.S. 130 (1967).

Branzburg v. Hayes, 408 U.S. 665 (1972).

Curtis Publishing Co. v. Butts, 388 U.S. 130 (1967).

Gannett v. DePasquale, 443 U.S. 368 (1979).

Gertz v. Robert Welch, Inc., 418 U.S. 323 (1974).

Green v. Alton Telegraph Printing Co., 107 Ill. App. 3d 755, 438 N.E. 2d 203 (1982).

Hutchinson v. Proxmire, 443 U.S. 111 (1979).

In re Farber, 394 A. 2d 330 (N.J. 1978).

Irvin v. Dowd, 366 U.S. 717 (1961).

Nebraska Press Association v. Stuart, 427 U.S. 539 (1976).

New York Times v. Sullivan, 376 U.S. 254 (1964).

Philadelphia Newspapers, Inc. v. Hepps, 475 U.S. 767 (1986).

Richmond Newspapers v. Virginia, 448 U.S. 555 (1980).

Rosenbloom v. Metromedia, Inc., 403 U.S. 29 (1971).

Sharon v. Time, Inc., 575 F. Supp. 1162 (D.C. N.Y., 1985).

Sheppard v. Maxwell, 384 U.S. 333 (1966).

Time, Inc. v. Firestone, 424 U.S. 448 (1976).

Periodicals

Anonymous. (1982, January-February). Romanticism revisited (Letter to the editor). *Columbia Journalism Review*, p. 65.

Boles, P. D. (1985, April). The elements of your personal writing style. *Writer's Digest*, pp. 24–28.

Donovan, R. J. (1985, July). Logging on. *Writer's Digest*, pp. 45–47.

Larson, E. (1985, February 13). Working at home: Is it freedom or a life of flabby loneliness? *The Wall Street Journal*, p. 33.

McKinney, D. (1983, September). How to make your articles sparkle. *Writer's Digest,* pp. 28–32.

Metro, G. (1981, February 28–March 1). Special on styles, priced to sell, *Weekend Northwestern,* p. A-7.

O'Malley, C. (1985, March). Writing smarter. *Personal Computing,* pp. 51–54.

Palmer, T. G. (1985, January 10). Uncle Sam's ever-expanding P.R. machine. *The Wall Street Journal,* p. 26.

Provost, G. (1983). Rapid transit. *Writer's Yearbook,* pp. 74–77, 126.

Rippis, A. K. (1988, October). Consider part-time work. *The Quill,* pp. 29–31.

Whitman, A. (1977, September). Alden Whitman: 11 years on the death watch. *More,* pp. 12, 14, 15.

Author Index

Subject Index